# Readers' Theater

## Volume Two - *20 plays*

# *Famous People*

*Author: Lois F. Roets* Ed.D.

Topics:

Susan B. Anthony

Authors & Fictional Characters They Created

Conquerors of Yellow Fever

Marie Curie

Decade of the 1950s

Amelia Earhart

Fighters of Bacterial Infection

First Ladies

Gandhi

Robert E. Lee

Abraham Lincoln

Men Who Supported Causes

Named After People

People Associated with Religions

People Who Improved Communications

Psychologists

Storytellers

U.S. Presidential Trivia

Women Artists

Women Who Supported Causes

# Readers' Theater
## *Volume Two:* **Famous People**

## Table of Content

ISBN: 0-911943-30-7     © Lois F. Roets Ed.D. 1992

**Leadership Publishers Inc.**
Post Office Box 8358
Des Moines, Iowa 50301 - 8358

# *Dedication*

*These plays are dedicated
to everyone who had the courage
to make this world a better place.*

# Introduction
*(Instructor's Manual)*

## Basic Information about Readers' Theater

In regular theater, there are costumes, sets, and properties to help the performers interpret the writer's script. Readers' theater does not use costumes or properties - unless a particular group of performers wishes to wear a hat, an article of clothing, or an object that identifies the role the reader is portraying. Identification tags may be worn or placed in front of each reader.

Readers' Theater has only **words** to convey messages. Words alone carry the story. It is up to the readers to enhance the story with expressive, interpretive reading of the lines. This enhancement is accomplished through:

√ tone of voice,

√ rate of speaking,

√ emphasis of words,

√ pauses, and

√ response to words spoken by other readers.

## How to Use this Collection of Plays

Read the plays as written.
Change them to represent other viewpoints.
Adapt them to meet your needs.
*(Wide margins allow for this editing.)*
Write your own plays.

## Who Should Use These Scripts?

Teachers and students interested in:

➡ *drama,*

✤ *public speaking/reading,*

⚥ *reading classes,*

☆ *language arts classes,*

♀ *social studies classes,*

➡ *counselors who want to provide outlets for student emotions,*

♣ *student and youth groups who need activities for meetings, weekend retreats, camping trips and related activities.*

# Susan B. Anthony

*Cast  - The following are female parts: Anthony, Stanton, and Chorus*
*Chorus - any number*
*Narrator One*
*Narrator Two*
*Susan B. Anthony*
*Elizabeth Cady Stanton*
*Historian One*
*Historian Two*

*Modifications you may wish to mak:.*
*Add information - dates & people - who played a part*
*in your geographic area.*

| | |
|---|---|
| **Narrator One:** | Today's play is about Susan B. Anthony - a woman whose efforts made it possible for women to vote. |
| **Chorus:** | Susan B., Susan B., Thanks for getting the vote for me. |
| **Narrator Two:** | Susan B. Anthony was the daughter of Daniel and Lucy Anthony.  The Anthony household was a Quaker household.  They followed the "plain living" lifestyle. |
| **Narrator One:** | "Plain living" meant that there was no music or toys in the Anthony household. |
| **Chorus:** | No music?  No toys? What did she do for fun? |
| **Historian One:** | She had the great outdoors as her playground. She had brothers and sisters and the outdoors of Adams, Massachusetts. |
| **Historian Two:** | Besides playing outside and with her brothers and sisters, she baked bread, quilted, sewed, and helped with the family laundry. |
| **Chorus:** | Was she a happy child?  Did her parents love her? |

| | |
|---|---|
| Historian One: | Her parents and her family loved her.<br>She had a secure loving family life. |
| Chorus: | Susan B., Susan B.,<br>Thanks for getting the vote for me. |
| Narrator One: | The Anthony household also supported major reforms, such as the antislavery and temperance movements. The temperance movement was an effort to abolish all alcoholic beverages. |
| Narrator Two: | Susan B. Anthony did not have a childhood filled with toys and music but she did grow up in a secure home that valued and cherished personal freedom and human rights. |
| Historian One: | She taught school from 1839-1849.<br>She joined the temperance movement. |
| Historian Two: | By age 28, she no longer was following the strict plain living of the Quaker way of life. She was an independent school teacher. She wore colorful clothes and a fancy bonnet. |
| Chorus: | Susan B., Susan B.,<br>Thanks for getting the vote for me. |
| Narrator One: | In 1851, she met Elizabeth Cady Stanton - a leader in the women's rights movement. |
| Narrator Two: | The two became friends and co-workers in the area of human rights - particularly the right for women to vote. |
| Anthony: | Good evening, Mrs. Stanton. My name is Susan B. Anthony. I am interested in the work you are doing to secure the right to vote for women. |
| Stanton: | I am equally happy to meet you, Miss Susan Anthony. Your reputation for hard work and success in organizing people and meetings is well known. |
| Anthony: | Since we are both working for the same causes, perhaps we should work together. Together we can be more effective and efficient than if we labored alone. |

Stanton:    Well said.  My home serves as headquarters for women's rights. You will be welcome at all times.

Anthony:    Women must have the right to vote.  Women take care of families.  Women are responsible people. Responsible people should have the right to vote.

Stanton:    Women's suffrage is a must.  Until we have the right to vote, we will be powerless.  Another cause we must support is the right for married women to own property.

Narrator One:    At that time, all property was listed in the man's name.

Narrator Two:    If a husband died, the house the wife lived in with her children did not belong to her.  Women were powerless and at the mercy of the laws and lawyers.

Historian One:    The year, 1876, was the centennial of the birth of of the United States.  Susan B. Anthony organized and led demonstrations.

Historian Two:    The demonstrators said that women should have the same constitutional rights that men had - which included the right to vote and to own property.

Historian One:    The nation's celebration was held in Philadelphia. Anthony and her demontrators were not allowed in Independence Hall.  You needed a pass to get in and Anthony did not have one.

Historian Two:    She did get a pass because her brother worked as a newspaper reporter.  Through her brother's efforts, she secured a press pass to enter the hall.

Historian One:    As you may have guessed, once inside the hall, she was not a quiet little mouse that no one saw or heard.

Historian Two:    As soon as she entered the Hall, she took over the stage. She loudly read the Declaration of Women's Rights. Then she proudly walked out.

Anthony:    The world cannot survive, and our nation cannot grow if half of its population - women - are denied voting power.

| | |
|---|---|
| Stanton: | The struggle is long but it is necessary. We shall go on. |
| Anthony: | We shall go on. Our next step is to call for an International Council of Women. |
| Stanton: | The purpose of this meeting will be to strengthen the position that the rights of women in any part of the world affects the position of women in every other part of the world. |
| Chorus: | Susan B., Susan B., Thanks for getting the vote for me. |
| Historian Two: | It took a long time for women to have the right to vote. The first meeting on the concerns of women was held in Seneca Falls, New York, in 1848. |
| Narrator One: | In 1852, Anthony attended a temperance rally in Albany, New York. She was not allowed to speak because she was a woman. |
| Narrator Two: | Her well-regulated childhood served her well. For when disappointment came, as it often did, she could put aside her own feelings and keep moving forward. |
| Narrator One: | The rights of women to vote and to own property were not the only problems facing the country. The Civil War, the North against the South, was fought from 1861-1865. |
| Narrator Two: | You will remember that the Anthony family was against slavery. |
| Anthony: | Slavery is wrong. So long as anyone is a slave, no one is really free. |
| Historian One: | Anthony was deeply disappointed after the Civil War. |
| Historian Two: | She was disappointed because supporters of the 15th amendment gave blacks the rights to vote - but not women. |

| | |
|---|---|
| Anthony: | Every responsible adult has the right and obligation to vote. That goal is my intent and that is my resolve. |
| Stanton: | It was in 1969, 4 years after the end of the Civil War, that Susan B and I formed the National Woman Suffrage Association. |
| Anthony: | We will have the right to vote. We will. |
| Stanton: | We will indeed. It may take a while, but we will have the vote. |
| Historian One: | Susan voted in the 1872 election. She was arrested and fined $100 because voting by women was illegal. |
| Historian Two: | She never paid the fine and no further action was taken against her. |
| Anthony: | I voted in 1872 and am proud of it. I had to take dramatic steps to get people's attention to a cause. |
| Historian Two: | Susan B. Anthony also supported equal educational opportunities for women. The University of Rochester would not admit women. |
| Historian One: | The university had many objections. The final objection was that it would cost too much money to admit women. |
| Anthony: | I offered my life insurance to guarantee the funds to cover the cost of admitting women. |
| Narrator One: | What happened? |
| Narrator Two: | Did the women get to go to college? |
| Anthony: | Yes. But the efforts to admit women took a toll on me. On the day the women were admitted, I suffered a stroke. I had to turn over some of the responsibility for the cause of women's rights to others. |
| Historian One: | She continued to work for women's right to vote. |

Historian Two:      After her stroke, Carrie Chapman Catt lead
the organization.

Narrator One:      Susan B. Anthony died in 1906, fourteen years before
the 19th amendment. The 19th amendment to the
Constitution gave U.S. women the right to vote.

Narrator Two:      The world mourned her death. Thousands of
mourners paid last respects to Susan B. Anthony
as she lay in state.

Historian One:      Twelve women dressed in white kept a
vigil around the casket.

Historian Two:      At the funeral, the honor bearers were women
students from the University of Rochester.

Historian One:      In the eulogy, the Reverend Anna Howard Shaw
spoke of Susan B. Anthony's legacy. Reverend Shaw
said that people who leave a legacy, such as
Miss Anthony, do not die. Their spirits live on.

Narrator One:      And in Susan B. Anthony's case, her spirit does live on.

Narrator Two:      Her spirit is living in every woman who
has the right to vote.

Historian Two:      In 1920, women secured the right to vote.
That was fourteen years after Anthony died.

Historian One:      In 1979, the U.S. government issued a coin bearing
her image. She was the first women to be pictured
on a U.S. coin used in general circulation.

Anthony:      So long as the rights of any people are denied,
none of us is free.

Chorus:      Susan B., Susan B.,
Thanks for getting the vote for me.

*The End*

# Authors and the Fictional People They Created

*Cast*
  *Reader*
  *Librarian*
  *Author*
  *Fictional Character*

*Modifications you may wish to make:*
  *Reassign lines for more readers.*
  *Put on display books referred to in this play.*
  *Invite an author as guest speaker to explain*
  *how he/she creates characters.*

Librarian:   The library is the place to find interesting people.
             Today's play is about authors who created interesting
             fictional people for their stories.

Reader:      If I like one book by an author, I usually like
             more books by the same author.  Why is that?

Librarian:   That's because you and the author agree
             on what makes people interesting.

Reader:      Let's get started.  I'm anxious to see which
             authors and fictional people I'll meet.

Librarian:   The authors will introduce themselves and
             the characters they created. Our first author
             is Herman Melville.

Author:      My name is Herman Melville.  I created
             Captain Ahab in my book Moby Dick.

Character:   Captain Ahab wanted to capture the white
             whale named Moby Dick. Ahab risked lives
             of people but he never got Moby Dick.

Author:      Lewis Carroll is my name.  I created Alice,
             of Alice in Wonderland.

Character:    Alice enters Wonderland by following a White Rabbit
                down a hole in the ground.  She gets smaller and larger.
                She also meets the Mad Hatter and the Queen of Hearts.

Author:       I am Sir Arthur Conan Doyle, an English author
                who created Sherlock Holmes and Dr. Watson.

Character:    Sherlock had great powers of memory, deduction,
                and observation.  He would take great risks and
                do experiments to prove theories.

Author:       You know me as Mark Twain.  My real name
                is Samuel Clemens.  You probably recognize
                Tom Sawyer and Huckleberry Finn.  Those are
                two fictional people I created.

Character:    Huckleberry Finn ran away from his father by going
                down the river with Jim, a runaway slave. Tom Sawyer
                led a different sort of life.  He was an adventurous boy
                who tried to outwit his Aunt Polly.

Author:       Charles Dickens is my name.  I wrote many
                stories which profiled the society of my time.
                My best-known character is Scrooge - from
                my story,  A Christmas Carol.

Character:    Scrooge was a stingy, unfeeling sort of person.
                His view of Christmas, at the beginning of the
                story, is "Bah, humbug!".  By the end of the story,
                Scrooge joins the rest of the human race in his
                attitude towards the feast of Christmas.

Author:       My name is Mary Wollstonecraft Shelley.  I created
                Dr. Victor Frankenstein, who created another monster.
                Did you know that I am really a very nice person?
                People think I must be strange because the fictional
                characters I created were strange.

Character:    Dr. Frankenstein creates a manlike monster from
                parts of dead bodies.  The monster is brought to life
                through electrical charges.  It is large and strong.

**Author:**      My real name was Theodor Seuss Geisel.
You know me by my pen name, Dr. Seuss.

**Character:**   The Grinch, the Cat in the Hat, Horton, and many
other characters fill the pages of Dr. Seuss's books.
Seuss characters and books are easily recognized.

**Author:**      Jonathan Swift is my name.  I wrote satire.  My stories
point out the weakness of society by making fun of it.

**Character:**   Swift created many of us: the Lilliputians - a group of
six-inch people; the Brobdingnagians - a group of giants;
and Yahoos - a group of mute laborers.  He also created
a land where horses are more intelligent than human beings .

**Reader:**      Would people get angry when Swift made fun of them?

**Librarian:**   Yes.  Authors often say things that people don't like.
Authors have a right to write what they want. The
reader has a right to read, or not to read, their works.

**Author:**      I am James Matthew Barrie - the creator of Peter Pan.
Peter Pan is the boy who doesn't want to grow up.

**Character:**   Peter Pan has a friend, Tinker Bell, and an
enemy, Captain Hook.  Captain Hook lost one
hand because a crocodile ate it.

**Author:**      Washington Irving is my name.  I tell adventurous
stories with fictional people you won't soon forget.

**Character:**   Rip Van Winkle - the man who slept so long, and
Ichabod Crane - the man chased by the Headless Horseman,
are two of us who came from Irving's imagination.

**Author:**      My name is Lyman Frank Baum.
I wrote The Wonderful Wizard of Oz.
For this story, I created Dorothy.

**Character:**  Dorothy is a little girl who is carried by a tornado
from Kansas to the enchanted land of Oz. Her
companions in Oz are the scarecrow who wants
a brain, the lion who wants courage, and the tin man
who wants a heart.

---

*---- optional insert ---*

*Most authors and characters presented in this play are
from literature enjoyed by many ages and interests.*

*Add authors and characters specific in appeal to the
group of readers doing this play.*

---

**Reader:**  Thanks to all authors for creating fictional
people that are interesting to meet. Authors,
keep writing. We'll keep reading.

**Librarian:**  I'll see all of you in the library.

*The End.*

Readers' Theater. CONQUERORS OF YELLOW FEVER page 1

*Vol. Two* - **11**

# Conquerors of Yellow Fever

*Cast:*

*Narrator*
*Medical Doctor*
*Carlos Juan Finlay*
*Max Theiler*
*Juan Guiteras*
*William Crawford Gorgas*
*Walter Reed*

*Modifications you may wish to make.*
*Display books about other "conquerors of disease."*
*Provide name tags to identify the readers.*
*Display a large map which includes the Panama Canal.*

Narrator:  Today's play is about people who conquered yellow fever.  Our guests will introduce themselves.

Finlay:  My name is Carlos Juan Finley. I am from Cuba.

Theiler:  My name is Max Theiler.
I am a South African research physician.

Guiteras:  I am Juan Guiteras, a native of Cuba.
My specialty is tropical diseases.

Gorgas:  I am William Crawford Gorgas.
I was born in Toulminville, Alabama.

Reed:  My name is Walter Reed. I am from Virginia.

Doctor:  I am a doctor. I represent all doctors who fight disease.

Narrator:  Thank you for being with us today.  We will
tell you about the conquerors of yellow fever.

Doctor:  Yellow fever is a viral disease.  It
has claimed the lives of many people.

Guiteras:  I was among the first to advance the idea that
children built up natural immunity to a disease.

Narrator:   How does that happen?

Guiteras:   The immunity comes when a young patient conquers mild bouts of the disease during childhood.

Doctor:   To conquer a disease, we have to know how it begins and how it progresses. Once that is understood, then we can develop ways to prevent the disease, and cure it once it gets started.

Narrator:   The question was raised: Why were there yellow fever epidemics in Veracruz, Mexico, and not in Mexico City?

Finlay:   I thought that mosquitoes might play a part in the disease. Veracruz is at sea level. Mosquitoes are everywhere. But Mexico City is 7,500 feet above sea level. Mosquitoes do not thrive at high altitudes. I suggested that yellow fever might be transmitted by the bite from a mosquito.

Reed:   I played a part in the experiments that proved yellow fever is transmitted by mosquitoes.

Narrator:   What did you do?

Reed:   I, and several other doctors and soldiers, volunteered to be infected by yellow fever germs.

Doctor:   These experiments proved, beyond doubt, that yellow fever was transmitted through the mosquito.

Narrator:   What happened?

Reed:   My colleagues and I were very sick.

Narrator:   Walter Reed died in those experiments. But the theory that mosquitoes play a part in the disease was correct.

Doctor:   The yellow fever disease could be carried from one person to another by the bite of certain mosquitoes. Some animals can also be infected. This is how it happens:

Finlay:     The mosquito first injects a fluid into the person
            it is biting.  This injection makes it possible for
            the mosquito to suck blood from the human, and
            take the blood into its own body.

Guiteras:   When that mosquito bites the next person,
            the disease is transmitted.

Theiler:    With this process, an infected mosquito can
            pass on yellow fever for the rest of its life.
            It can infect many people.

Narrator:   How do I know if I have yellow fever?
            What symptoms would I have?

Theiler:    Yellow fever's first symptoms are fever,
            headache, dizziness, and aching muscles.  The
            disease progresses no further - for some people.

Finlay:     For others, it gets worse,  The fever drops for a
            day or two.  Then it rises very high.  The kidneys
            are affected and the body is not purified.

Theiler:    When the kidneys do not remove impurities, the skin turns
            yellow - which gives the disease the name "yellow fever".

Guiteras:   The lining of the patient's stomach and gums bleed. Many die.

Doctor:     There are also many others who recover from
            these advanced stages.  If they recover, they will
            have lifelong immunity.

Theiler:    Immunity, or protection against disease, is an
            interesting process.  A person can become immune
            by having a mild case of the disease.

Finlay:     Once your body is attacked by a disease, your body
            fights it. If you survive the disease, you will
            probably be immune for the rest of your life.

Reed:       Now that it was known how the yellow fever
            spread, steps had to be taken to control it.

Guiteras:   Since the mosquito spreads the disease, the first
            step in controlling it was eliminating the breeding
            grounds for mosquitoes.

Gorgas:     And that's where I come into the picture.  The
            United States wanted to build a canal in Panama
            which would connect the Atlantic and the Pacific Oceans.
            *(If a map is on display, point to the Canal region, and the Atlantic & Pacific oceans.)*

Narrator:   The U.S. wanted the canal so that their ships would not have
            sail all the way around South America.  *(If a map is on display,
            show the route a ship would have to take to sail around South America.)*

Reed:       Many political agreements had to be reached between the
            United States and Panama.  After they were negotiated,
            one major problem remained in building the canal - disease.

Gorgas:     There were three major diseases that endangered the
            builders - yellow fever, malaria, and bubonic plague.

Doctor:     The mosquitoes carried and spread yellow fever and
            malaria.  The rats spread bubonic plague.

Gorgas:     In 1904, I was appointed chief sanitary officer of
            the Panama Canal Commission.  The first two years
            of canal building were devoted largely to clearing
            brush, draining swamps, and cutting out large areas
            of grass where the mosquitoes swarmed.

Doctor:     By 1906, Gorgas had wiped out yellow fever.
            The rats that caused bubonic plague in the
            Canal Zone were also eliminated.

Theiler:    In 1937, my colleagues and I developed a vaccine
            to control yellow fever.  The vaccine, along with
            control of breeding grounds for mosquitoes, has
            greatly reduced the risk of yellow fever.

Doctor:     The diseases of yellow fever, malaria and bubonic
            plague were now under control.  And they must be
            continuously kept under control.

Readers' Theater. CONQUERORS OF YELLOW FEVER page 5

*Vol. Two* - **15**

Narrator:  Walter Reed died as a result of the experiments to prove that yellow fever is carried by mosquitoes. He died so that others may live.

Doctor:  Walter Reed Medical Center in Washington D.C. is named after him.

Guiteras:  It took all of us to learn how to control yellow fever.

Finlay:  It is up to you *(motions to audience)* to apply what we have learned.

Reed:  Control breeding grounds for mosquitoes.

Theiler:  Get the immunizations you need.

Gorgas:  Keep living areas clean.

Doctor:  Stay healthy.

Narrator:  And so our play ends with two final words to our medical scientists.

Doctor:  Thank you.

Finley, Gorgas, Guiteras, Reed, and Theiler: You're welcome.

*The End*

# Marie Curie

*Cast*

*Marie Curie*
*Pierre Curie*
*Narrator One*
*Narrator Two*
*Chorus - represents the scientific community*

*Modifications you may wish to make:*
*Add more information about Marie Curie.*

| | |
|---|---|
| Marie Curie: | My name is Manya Sklodowska. You probably know me as Marie Curie - or Madame Curie. |
| Chorus: | Marie Curie was a scientist, a scholar, a Polish hero, and a physicist. We honor her today. |
| Marie Curie: | I was born on November 7, 1867, in Warsaw, Poland. |
| Narrator One: | At the time Dr. Curie was born, Poland was divided into German, Russian and Austrian sections. Marie was born in the Russian part of Poland. |
| Narrator Two: | The Polish people tried to be free but they did not succeed. After the revolts, the Russians suppressed Poland's religion, books, newspapers and even the Polish language. |
| Marie Curie: | My father was professor of mathematics and physics. He kept some of his scientific equipment in our house. I liked my father and liked the world of science. |
| Narrator One: | Marie was a bright child who learned to read by age four. She was noted for her great memory. |
| Narrator Two: | Her mother died when she was seven years of age. |

| | |
|---|---|
| <u>Chorus</u>: | Marie Curie was a loving daughter, a loyal patriot of Poland, and a scholar. We honor her today. |
| <u>Marie Curie</u>: | I always liked learning.  At sixteen, I graduated from high school - first in my class. |
| <u>Narrator One</u>: | She enter the Sorbonne in Paris, France.  She earned the License of Physical Sciences in 1893 - placing first in her class.  The following year, she earned a second license - in mathematics - placing second in her class. |
| <u>Narrator Two</u>: | It was also in 1894 that Marie first met Pierre Curie. |
| <u>Marie Curie</u>: | I first saw Pierre Curie standing near a door leading to the balcony. |
| <u>Pierre Curie</u>: | Up to this time, I had been solely devoted to my laboratory work.  I did not permit myself to become interested in women. |
| <u>Marie Curie</u>: | Pierre was unlike any man I had ever met. He was a scientist with a passion for science equal to mine.  His speech was slow and reflective. He was both grave and pleasant. |
| <u>Pierre Curie</u>: | Meeting Marie changed my life.  We had the same commitment to science. We shared the same interest in physics. |
| <u>Narrator One</u>: | Pierre and Marie Curie were married.  It was a marriage that combined love, friendship and professional achievements. |
| <u>Narrator Two</u>: | They talked about their work.  They shared their ideas, efforts, love and dreams. |
| <u>Marie Curie</u>: | We were very happy - with each other and with our work. |

Pierre Curie:        When our two daughters were born, our
                     happiness seemed complete.

Narrator One:        In 1893, Marie earned a doctorate in physics.
                     That same year, she and Pierre, along with
                     Henri Becquerel, were awarded the Nobel
                     Prize in physics.

Narrator Two:        The award was given for their work with
                     uranium and radioactive materials.

Marie Curie:         My happiness, and that of our daughters,
                     was radically disrupted when Pierre was
                     run over and killed on a Paris street.

Chorus:              Marie was greatly saddened.
                     She expressed her sorrow and
                     devotion by continuing his work.
                     We honor that dedication today.

Narrator One:        Marie directed all her efforts to complete
                     the work she and Pierre had started.
                     She assumed his directorship of the
                     physics laboratory.

Narrator Two:        She took over Pierre's teaching assignment
                     at the Sorbonne.  She was the first woman
                     to teach there.

Marie Curie:         The Swedish Academy of Sciences honored me
                     with a second Nobel Prize - this time in chemistry -
                     for the discoveries of radium and polonium.
                     I named polonium after my native Poland.

Narrator One:        As a result of prolonged exposure to radioactive
                     materials, Marie Curie died of anemia in 1934.

Narrator Two:        In the following year, 1935, Marie's daughter and
                     her husband received the Nobel Prize in physics
                     for the ability to make artificial radioactivity.

Narrator One:    It is the one and only case in history where a mother and a daughter have both won Nobel Prizes in science.

Narrator Two:    Marie Curie was an extraordinarily talented scientist. The world is lucky she was determined to use her talents.

Chorus:    Marie Curie was a scientist,
a scholar, a Polish hero, and a physicist.
We honor her today.

*The End*

# A Decade of People & Events - the 1950s

**1950s**

*Cast*

   *Calendar*
   *Historian One*
   *Historian Two*
   *Historian Three*
   *Historian Four*
   *Historian Five*

*Modifications you may wish to make:*
   *Add other information from the 1950s that you
   consider important to the readers using this play.*

*Suggestions for more plays:*
   *Another period of time or geographic location may be the focus of a play.*

---

**People mentioned in this play are:**

| | | | |
|---|---|---|---|
| Ball, Lucille | Bannister, Roger | Brown, Linda | Castro, Fidel |
| Christie, Agatha | Clark, Dick | Cochran, Jacqueline | Cousteau, Jacques-Yves |
| Crosby, Bing | Dior, Christian | Dlugi, Bertha | Egan, William |
| Elizabeth II, Queen | Geisel, Theodor | George VI, King | Hillary, Sir Edmund |
| Kennedy, John F. | Kroc, Ray | MacArthur, Douglas | Mays, Willie |
| McDonald, Mac & Dick | Norgay, Tenzing | Parks, Rosa | Pasternak, Boris |
| Pele | Pollock, Jackson | Pope John XXIII | Presley, Elvis |
| Quinn, William F. | Roncalli, Angelo Guiseppe | Ronstadt, Linda | Sabin, Dr. Albert |
| Salk, Dr. Jonas | Schulz, Charles M. | Seuss, Dr. | Shoemaker, Willie |
| Simon & Garfunkel | Sinatra, Frank | Stalin, Joseph | Tolkien, J.R.R. |
| Truman, Harry | Winston, Harry | Wonder, Stevie | Wright, Frank Lloyd |

---

**One:**      A decade is a period of ten years.

**Calendar:**  This play will review the decade of the '50s: 1950 to 1959.

**Two:**      We'll fill you in on people and events for each year.

**Calendar:**  1950.

**Three:**     A survey of 11-15 year-olds revealed that they spent as
             much time watching television as they did going to school.

Readers' Theater. DECADE OF THE 1950s  page 2

*Vol. Two* - **21**

Four:        Charles M. Schulz created Peanuts - that
lovable cartoon character.

Five:        Frank Sinatra replaced Bing Crosby as
America's most popular singer.

One:        Artist Jackson Pollock painted "splashy"
and "tossed" pictures. These were pictures
that looked like the paint had been splashed
or tossed on the canvas.

Calendar:    1951.

Two:        Jacques-Yves Cousteau, inventor of the
Aqualung, perfected the underwater television
camera. The world of the ocean could now be
seen on our television sets.

Three:      Willie Mays started playing professional baseball.
In 27 times at bat, he got only one hit. Then he started
to hit and run. He was named Rookie of the Year.

Four:        President Harry Truman dismissed Douglas
MacArthur as Far East Commander. He was
dismissed because he made public statements
that disagreed with the United Nations and
the United States Government's defense plans.

Calendar:    1952.

Five:        King George VI of England died. His
daughter, Elizabeth, would become queen.

One:        Agatha Christie, the British mystery writer,
wrote the play, "The Mousetrap". It continues
its nonstop run - even to the 1990s.

Two:        "I Love Lucy," the popular television comedy,
made its debut. Comedienne Lucille Ball was
its star. The show is still a popular rerun.

*Vol. Two -* **22**

Readers' Theater. DECADE OF THE 1950s  page 3

1950s

Three:    Dick Clark and the "American Bandstand"
          was the first television show devoted to
          rock and roll.  Linda Ronstadt, Simon and
          Garfunkel, the Supremes, the Temptations
          and Stevie Wonder were on the show.

Calendar:  1953.

Four:     Elvis Presley made a record for his mother's
          birthday.  It was a simple beginning to fame.

Five:     On the political scene, Joseph Stalin died. Elizabeth
          was crowned as Queen Elizabeth II of England.

One:      John F. Kennedy married Jacqueline Bouvier.

Two:      Sir Edmund Hillary of New Zealand and his Sherpa
          guide, Tenzing Norgay, were the first to climb to the
          top of Mount Everest - the highest mountain in the world.

Three:    Jacqueline Cochran became the first woman to break
          the sound barrier.  She flew 760 miles an hour.

Calendar:  1954.

Four:     British athlete Roger Bannister ran the mile in less than
          four minutes - 3 minutes and 59.4 seconds, to be exact.

Five:     The Supreme Court ordered schools to open their
          classrooms to all children.  Linda Brown, a young
          black girl living in Topeka, Kansas, helped to make
          this possible.  She sued the Board of Education in
          Topeka when a local school refused to register her.

One:      Dr. Jonas Salk developed a vaccine to guard against polio.

Two:      J.R.R. Tolkien published <u>Lord of the Rings</u> .

Calendar:  1955.

**1950**s

Three:       Jockey Willie Shoemaker won his first Kentucky Derby.
             At birth, he weighed only 2 and one-half pounds.  He
             wasn't expected to live.  His grandma made sure he did.

Four:        The first McDonald's restaurant opened in Chicago.
             Ray Kroc bought the rights to the marketing plan from
             the McDonald boys, Mac and Dick.

Five:        Rosa Parks, a black woman, refused to sit in the back
             of a city bus in Montgomery, Alabama.  The civil rights
             movement for blacks was moved forward.

Calendar:    1956.

One:         Bertha Dlugi invented a bird diaper so her bird
             could fly freely round the house.

Two:         "Pele," the soccer player, was discovered. He
             played for the national team of his country - Brazil.

Three:       Dr. Albert Sabin perfected a polio vaccine that could be
             taken by mouth - rather than by hypodermic needle.

Calendar:    1957.

Four:        Random House Publishing Company published Theodor
             Geisel's first book.  You'll recognize Geisel by his pen
             name: Dr. Seuss. This first book was <u>The Cat in the Hat</u>.

Five:        The French fashion designer, Christian Dior,
             died.  But the Dior look and name remains a legend.

One:         The Sony Corporation marketed the first
             pocket-sized transistor radio.

Calendar:    1958.

Two:         Angelo Guiseppe Roncalli of Bergamo, Italy
             was elected head of the Roman Catholic Church.
             He chose the name of Pope John XXIII.

**1950**s

Three:       Doctor Zhivago, a story by the Russian novelist
             Boris Pasternak, was the top-selling novel.

Four:        Jeweler Harry Winston donated the 112-carat
             blue Hope diamond to the Smithsonian Institution.
             Owners of that stone had a history of ill fortune.

Calendar:    1959.

Five:        The Barbie Doll was introduced by the Mattell Corporation.

One:         Alaska became the 49th state.
             Its first governor was William Egan.

Two:         Hawaii became the 50th state.
             William F. Quinn became its first governor.

Three:       Fidel Castro seized power in Cuba.

Four:        The architect Frank Lloyd Wright died
             but his style of building remains with us.

Five:        The first transatlantic television show was transmitted.
             Quick access to information from and to many parts
             of the world was now possible.

Calendar:    December 31st closed the year 1959,
             and the decade of the '50s.
             And so this play is ended.


*The End*

# Amelia Earhart

*Cast:*
Amelia Earhart
Narrator One
Narrator Two
Reporter One
Reporter Two
Researcher One
Researcher Two
Inquiring Mind One
Inquiring Mind Two

*Modifictions you may wish to make:*
Combine or re-distribute the parts of Narrator, Researcher,
Reporter and Inquiring Mind to accommodate more or fewer readers.

| | |
|---|---|
| Amelia: | My name is Amelia Earhart. Thank you for inviting me to your class today. |
| Research One: | Amelia Earhart was a pilot - a woman pilot - at a time in history when all pilots drew special attention. Women pilots drew more attention. |
| Research Two: | You've probably heard of Amelia Earhart. She's the woman who wanted to fly around the world at the equator. |
| Research One: | The equator is the longest route around the planet and the most difficult because of air currents and clouds above the equator. |
| Research Two: | Her plane vanished near Howland Island in the Pacific Ocean. No absolute recovery of the plane was made. No absolute explanation of what happened to Amelia Earhart and her navigator, Fred Noonan, has been made. |
| Narrator One: | That's the end of the story. We should start at the beginning. |
| Inq. Mind One: | What's the beginning? |

| | |
|---|---|
| Narrator Two: | Amelia Earhart's story starts in Atchison, Kansas, and the year 1897. |
| Inq.Mind Two: | What kind of a girl was she? |
| Research One: | Amelia had one younger sister, Muriel.  They were considered "unladylike" because the girls' parents allowed them to do things traditionally done by boys? |
| Amelia: | I must have been a horrid girl.  I wanted a sled - the same kind that the boys would get - sturdy and very fast. |
| Inq.Mind One: | What other kinds of things did the Earhart girls do that other girls in Kansas did not do? |
| Research Two: | They played baseball, explored caves, and walked on stilts. They fished and collected insects, worms and toads. |
| Inq.Mind Two: | Girls today do that all the time. |
| Research Two: | Yes, they do. And they are encouraged to do so.  But it wasn't always that way. |
| Amelia: | I talked my friends into building a roller coaster. |
| Inq.Mind One: | Did it  work? |
| Amelia: | Not really.  But it was great fun. |
| Inq.Mind One: | The Earhart girls were lucky that their parents were so tolerant and encouraging. |
| Reporter One: | My reporter's notebook provides this information: Amelia's mother was the daughter of wealthy influential parents.  Her mother, Amy Otis Earhart, was the first woman to climb to the top of Pike's Peak in Colorado. |
| Narrator One: | You can now understand why Amelia was encouraged to play as she wished and to test the limits of her mind and body. |

| | |
|---|---|
| Reporter Two: | My reporter's notebook provides this information about Amelia's father: Edwin Earhart was a son of a minister. He was a lawyer for the railroads and was frequently away on business. |
| Inq.Mind Two: | Did Amelia travel with him? |
| Reporter Two: | No, but her mother often went with him. The girls would stay for long periods of time with their grandparents - the Otis grandparents in Atchison. |
| Inq.Mind One: | Did Amelia like it at her grandparents? |
| Reporter One: | Yes. Her grandparents were influential people. She met and learned how to mingle with people of power and prestige. She also had the advantage of access to her grandfather's extensive library. |
| Inq.Mind Two: | Did she read a lot? Was she good at school work? |
| Reporter One: | She read many, many books and was a good student. She knew how to study. |
| Inq.Mind One: | What other things do you know about Amelia's early childhood and about her family? |
| Amelia: | I'd like to answer that. My childhood had one great difficulty. |
| Inq.Mind Two: | What was that? |
| Amelia: | My father changed jobs quite a few times and we had to move a lot. Sometimes that was all right. At other times, it was difficult. |
| Inq.Mind One: | Why did her father change jobs so many times? |
| Reporter One: | Her father had a problem with alcohol. He couldn't keep a job because alcohol interfered with his work. |
| Amelia: | Don't talk about that. Let's talk about airplanes. |

| | |
|---|---|
| <u>Narrator One</u>: | Amelia was ten years old when she saw her first airplane.  It was at the Iowa State Fair. |
| <u>Narrator Two</u>: | The plane was a biplane - that is, it had double wings. It was built of wire, wood and oiled canvas. |
| <u>Inq.Mind Two</u>: | I've seen pictures of biplanes.  Some of those pictures show the pilot sitting out in open air. |
| <u>Narrator One</u>: | Biplane pilots wore leather jackets and goggles for protection. |
| <u>Inq.Mind One</u>: | When did Amelia start to fly? |
| <u>Research One</u>: | She met four injured pilots while working as a nurse's aide in a hospital in Toronto, Canada. These men were military pilots. The year was 1917. |
| <u>Research Two</u>: | These pilots made a big impression on Amelia.  They told about their activities in war and about the planes they flew. |
| <u>Amelia</u>: | I listened to these pilots and I watched pilots perform at Toronto air shows.  I then understood that planes could fight battles, take people from place to place, and entertain people. |
| <u>Inq.Mind Two</u>: | And that's when you became a pilot? |
| <u>Amelia</u>: | No, but from that time on, planes were the major focus of my life. |
| <u>Narrator One</u>: | Amelia worked for a telephone company to pay for flying lessons from Neta Snook, the first woman to graduate from the Curtiss School of Aviation. |
| <u>Narrator Two</u>: | In 1922 she got her pilot's license. |
| <u>Reporter One</u>: | Amelia spent a lot of time in the air.  She taught herself to land with the engine turned off. |
| <u>Inq.Mind One</u>: | Why would she want to fly or land with the plane's engine turned off? |

Reporter One:        She knew there would be times when she'd
                     have to land without power from the engine.

Inq.Mind Two:        When would that be?

Reporter One:        Sometimes the engine would die - all by itself.
                     Then Amelia would have to land without power.
                     There are times when plane engines catch on fire.
                     Then she'd have to shut off the engine to keep
                     the whole plane from exploding or burning.

Reporter Two:        The ability to land a plane without an engine running
                     saved her life, and her plane, many times.

Amelia:              The world of planes was my world.  I enjoyed flying,
                     improving my abilities and trying to set new records.

Reporter One:        She did set many records.

Narrator One:        In 1922 she secured her pilot's license.

Reporter Two:        In that same year Amelia set the woman's altitude
                     record - 14,000 feet or almost 3 miles. When she
                     reached that height, her engine quit.  She landed safely.
                     The plane was an open-cockpit, single-engine biplane.

Narrator Two:        June, 1929.

Research One:        First woman to fly across the Atlantic as a passenger.

Narrator One:        July, 1930.

Research Two:        Set woman's speed record of 181 miles per hour.
                     This flight was made in a single-engine monoplane.

Narrator Two:        February, 1931.

Reporter One:        Married G.P. Putnam, a publisher.  She agreed to marry
                     Putnam after he signed an agreement that stated if they
                     found no happiness together within the first year of
                     marriage,  he would release her from the marriage.

| | |
|---|---|
| <u>Inq. Mind One</u>: | Were they happy? |
| <u>Reporter One</u>: | It appears to be so - for they remained together. |
| <u>Narrator One</u>: | May, 1932. |
| <u>Reporter Two</u>: | First woman to fly solo across the Atlantic. The plane was a single engine monoplane. That flight also set the woman's distance record of 2,026.5 miles. |
| <u>Narrator Two</u>: | June, 1932. |
| <u>Reporter Two</u>: | Amelia Earhart received the National Geographic Society's Special Medal - the first woman to do so. |
| <u>Narrator One</u>: | July, 1932. |
| <u>Research One</u>: | Amelia received the Distinguished Flying Cross Award - the first civilian to receive it. |
| <u>Narrator Two</u>: | August, 1932. |
| <u>Research Two</u>: | Amelia set the woman's nonstep transcontinental speed record from Los Angeles, California, to Newark, New Jersey. The time was 19 hours, 5 minutes. |
| <u>Narrator One</u>: | July, 1933. |
| <u>Research Two</u>: | Amelia broke her own transcontinental nonstop flight record of 19 hours and five minutes with a new record of 17 hours and 7 minutes. |
| <u>Reporter One</u>: | Flying was her life. She set and broke records, knew Charles Lindbergh, visited with presidents and gave speeches around the country. |
| <u>Narrator Two</u>: | 1937 - before her final trip, Amelia said: |
| <u>Amelia</u>: | I have a feeling that there is just one more good flight left in my system, and I hope this flight is it." |

| | |
|---|---|
| Narrator One: | June, 1937. |
| Amelia: | I want to fly around the world - at the equator. Here are my plans: I'll leave Oakland, California, and fly to Honolulu, Hawaii. Then I'll go onto Howland Island in the central Pacific, Port Darwin in Northern Australia, Africa by way of Saudi Arabia. I'll cross the south Atlantic at Brazil and fly back to the U.S. |
| Research One: | The most dangerous part of that trip was landing at tiny Howland Island in the central Pacific. The island was only two miles long and one-half mile wide. The island jutted only twenty feet above the water. |
| Research Two: | Howland Island was a tiny speck of land in an ocean of moving, churning water. And Pacific waters and islands are often covered with clouds. |
| Reporter One: | There was another major danger: the plane could be shot down by the Japanese if it flew too close to the Caroline, Mariana, and Marshall Islands. |
| Reporter Two: | There were hints that the Japanese were using these islands to build up military strength. |
| Narrator Two: | July, 1937. |
| Research One: | Amelia started her flight. Fred Noonan was her navigator. All went reasonably well until she neared Howland Island. |
| Research Two: | The last radio message received from Amelia Earhart and her navigator, Fred Noonan, was "We are circling." |
| Reporter Two: | Her husband, waiting in San Francisco to welcome her home, appealed to the Japanese Consulate to aid in the search. No one replied. |
| Reporter One: | Earhart and Noonan, and the Electra plane she flew, were never officially seen again. |

| | |
|---|---|
| <u>Inq. Mind One</u>: | What happened? |
| <u>Inq. Mind Two</u>: | I read in a book that people saw Earhart and Noonan. I also read that they were captured and then killed. |
| <u>Research One</u>: | Several theories are suggested: Theory One: She was captured and executed by the Japanese because she was thought to be spying for the U.S. on Japanese military buildup in the Pacific. |
| <u>Research Two</u>: | Theory Two: Navigator Noonan was unable to navigate because of clouds and a storm in the Howland Island area. The area does have frequent storms and dense clouds. And remember: the island was very small. |
| <u>Reporter One</u>: | Theory Three: They crashed and died. Or they crash-landed but died from lack of water on Nikumaroro, an island near Howland. |
| <u>Reporter Two</u>: | Theory Four: They were captured and Amelia died of dysentery and Noonan was executed. |
| <u>Research One</u>: | And who knows how many more theories will be developed? Until conclusive evidence is secured, the mystery of this courageous woman pilot, her navigator, and her famous flight will remain an unsolved mystery. |
| <u>Research Two</u>: | But there is one part of the story that is not a mystery. That part clearly states that Amelia Earhart challenged herself to use every talent she had. |
| <u>Reporter One</u>: | Discover the talents you have. |
| <u>Reporter Two</u>: | Develop them fully. |
| <u>Narrator One</u>: | And, on that suggestion, this story will end. |

*The End*

# Fighters Against Bacterial Infections

*Cast*
> Doctor One
> Doctor Two
> Historian One
> Historian Two
> Joseph Lister
> Louis Pasteur
> Ignaz Semmelweis

*Modifications you may wish to make:*
> *Display books about medical achievers and achievements.*

**Semmelweis:** My name is Ignaz Semmelweis, a Hungarian doctor. I was born in Hungary in 1818. I am pleased to introduce myself and this play.

**Pasteur:** I am Louis Pasteur. I was born in France in 1822.

**Lister:** I am Joseph Lister. I was born in 1827 in England.

**Doctor One:** These three scientists *(nods to Semmelweis, Lister & Pasteur)* and our two historians *(nods to Historian One and Historian Two)* will review with you the discovery and control of bacteria - the main cause of infection.

**Doctor Two:** It is because of the combined efforts of Semmelweis, Pasteur, and Lister that the nature and control of infection is understood.

**Historian One:** Ignaz Semmelweis was the leader. At a Vienna hospital, 12 out of every 100 mothers were dying because of infections following childbirth.

**Semmelweis:** This was outrageous that so many women would die giving birth to children. How could society continue with this high number of deaths?

**Historian Two:** Dr. Semmelweis reasoned that the infections which caused death were being spread by the unclean hands of the doctors themselves.

Semmelweis:    If we doctors had very clean hands when we helped mothers give birth, fewer mothers would die. I just knew that unclean hands were causing the infections which caused death.

Doctor One:    As you may well imagine, doctors did not like to be told that they were causing the infections that killed their own patients.

Historian One:    Doctors were outraged. They told Semmelweis he was wrong. Doctors cured patients - not killed patients.

Semmelweis:    I was not running a popularity contest among my fellow doctors. So I continued to stress that clean hands were a necessity. Childbirth should happen in antiseptic conditions.

Historian Two:    Semmelweis was an outcast among doctors. He died a disappointed man. But his theory was correct.

Doctor Two:    In the year of Semmelweis' death, Joseph Lister proved Semmelweis was right.

Doctor One:    Today we recognize that the work of Ignaz Semmelweis, a Hungarian doctor, played a major role in safe childbirth for mothers and babies.

Pasteur:    I am the next step in understanding and controlling the battle against bacterial infections.

Historian One:    Pasteur was born in 1822, in France, a son of a tanner. He was a slow but steady student. Pasteur proved beyond a doubt that bacteria caused infections.

Historian Two:    Pasteur was not the first to discover bacteria but he was the first to prove its relationship with infections. Pasteur proved that bacteria live almost everywhere but their spread can be controlled.

Pasteur:              I developed a process called pasteurization
                      - the use of heat to kill germs. I applied this
                      method to preserve milk, beer, and food, since
                      bacteria can destroy all three products.

Doctor One:           How did you learn more about bacteria and infections?

Pasteur:              The first problem I set out to solve was the problem
                      the silk industry was experiencing. Something was
                      killing great numbers of silkworms.

Doctor Two:           Through extensive research, He showed that a bacterial
                      microbe was attacking the silkworm eggs. When these
                      eggs hatched, the disease grew and killed the worms.

Pasteur:              I showed that the disease could be controlled by
                      getting rid of the germ in the silkworm nurseries.
                      The silk industry was saved. And more proof was
                      added that it was microscopic bacteria that caused
                      infections, and these infections could cause death.

Historian One:        Pasteur proved that germs multiply in the body. This
                      new knowledge made vaccinations or immunizations possible.

Pasteur:              I showed that if bacterial microbes are weakened
                      in the laboratory, and then put into an animal's body,
                      that animal will develop an immunity to the microbe
                      or disease that the microbe causes.

Historian Two:        The principle of injecting weakened microbes into
                      the body to build the body's resistance is the principle
                      upon which vaccinations or immunizations is built.

Doctor One:           Vaccinations and immunizations have saved many
                      lives - in the past and in the present.

Pasteur:              I thought that we could control disease through
                      injections. I proved this theory by controlling and
                      eliminating anthrax - a disease in sheep. Later, I was
                      able to stop the growth of rabies in human beings.

Historian One:     Louis Pasteur had established landmark
information that could be applied to many
other situations. This information confirmed
that bacterial microbes cause disease.

Pasteur:     Bacteria are everywhere.  They can be
controlled if proper steps are taken.

Doctor Two:     Make sure you have all the immunizations you need.
If the shot hurts a little bit when you get immunized,
that is much less painful then the disease you could get.

Historian Two:     In 1868, a brain stroke partially paralyzed
Pasteur.  He continued to work as best as he
could until he died in 1895.

Doctor One:     In gratitude to Louis Pasteur, the Pasteur Institute
in Paris, France was founded in 1888.

Doctor Two:     It is a world center for the study, prevention,
and treatment of disease.  All of us are grateful
for the work of Louis Pasteur.

Lister:     My contribution followed the world of Louis Pasteur.
I have been called the father of antiseptic surgery.

Historian One:     Joseph Lister was born in England.  He was
educated and worked in Scotland and England.

Historian Two:     When Dr. Lister began his surgical work,
50% of surgery patients died as a result of
infection that followed surgery.

Lister:     After Louis Pasteur discovered that bacteria caused
infection, I realized that the formation of pus, a
sign of infection, was also due to germs and bacteria.

Historian One:     He first used carbolic acid sprays to kill germs in the air.

Lister:     This was somewhat effective but not as effective
as it could be. I knew of the work of Semmelweis
who contended that the unclean hands of doctors
spread infection.

| | |
|---|---|
| <u>Doctor One</u>: | Lister insisted on the use of antiseptics on hands, instruments, and dressings for all stages of surgery. |
| <u>Lister</u>: | The experiments showed immediate results by significantly reducing infections. |
| <u>Historian Two</u>: | His application of antiseptics so revolutionized surgery that surgery's whole history can be divided into two periods: before-Lister and after-Lister. |
| <u>Doctor Two</u>: | Death by infections for surgery patients fell to 3% or lower. |
| <u>Lister</u>: | My contribution to the field of surgery helped mankind.  It also showed that the work of one researcher builds upon the knowledge learned by other researchers. I stood on the shoulders of the giants: Semmelweis and Pasteur. |
| <u>Historian One</u>: | Lister was surgeon to Queen Victoria. He was the first medical man to be elevated to peerage by the British government. |
| <u>Historian Two</u>: | Sir Joseph Lister died in 1912. He left the world a better place by the contributions he made. |
| <u>All</u>: | Thanks to all medical doctors and scientists for all the improvements that have been made. |

*The End.*

# First Ladies

*Cast*

> *Calendar*
> *Newspaper Reporter*
> *First Lady - represents all First Ladies*
> *Narrator*

*Modifications you may wish to make:*

> Add other information about first ladies that may be of interest to the group.
> The Calendar could have cards listing the president's name and years
> of presidency. The First Lady could also have cards listing
> the name of the First lady.
> Assign the "First Lady" lines to more readers.

**Narrator:** The term "first lady" refers to the wife of a president. It is believed to have been used the first time in 1877.

**Reporter:** Reporters like to watch presidents and their wives. When our first woman president is elected, I'm certain we'll be just as anxious to watch the president and her husband - the first gentleman.

**Calendar:** Our play is a quick review of First Ladies.

**First Lady:** As First Lady, I will tell you just a bit about my personality, and a few recorded facts of history. Martha Washington is the first to be reviewed.

**Calendar:** Martha Washington was the wife of George Washington who held office from 1789-1797.

**First Lady:** I was the first to experience the impossibility of pleasing all people. Some people considered our entertainment too modest and some too extravagant. Many did not approve of theater outings which George and I enjoyed.

**Calendar:** Abigail Smith Adams was wife of John Adams who was President from 1797-1801.

*First Ladies* ☆ **First Ladies** ☆ *First Ladies* ☆

First Lady: John was your president and my husband. He appreciated my intelligence and political sense. I learned political sense from my grandfather, who was speaker of the Massachusetts House of Representatives.

Reporter: Thomas Jefferson's daughter served as hostess for the White House. His wife had died before he was elected to office.

Calendar: Dolley Payne Todd Madison, First Lady of James Madison, President from 1809-1817.

First Lady: I loved presiding at the White House parties. James and I were the first to give an inaugural ball. Over 400 guests attended.

Calendar: Elizabeth Kortright Monroe, First Lady of James Monroe, President from 1817 - 1825.

First Lady: The biggest problem I had as first lady was that I followed Dolley Madison. I knew what to do and how to act, but Dolley was just a favorite. And I wasn't as popular as she was. It was during this administration that the president's residence was painted white. It became the White House.

Narrator: The reporter and I are going to move us ahead by briefly summarizing some First Ladies' information.

Reporter: Louisa Johnson Adams was wife to John Quincy Adams. She always felt trapped in the White House.

Narrator: A relative performed the duties of hostess for Andrew Jackson as his wife had died.

Reporter: Anna Symmes Harrison was too ill to go with her husband, William Harrison, to his inauguration. She never lived in the White House, for her husband died exactly one month after he had taken the oath of office.

☆ *First Ladies* ☆ **First Ladies** ☆ *First Ladies* ☆

Calendar: Letitia Christian Tyler and Julia Gardiner Tyler served as First Ladies for John Tyler, president from 1841-1845.

First Lady: Each of us loved John Tyler and each of us bore seven of his children. Letitia preferred to stay in the background - relatively unnoticed. Julia liked to be noticed and hosted many parties.

Calendar: Sarah Childress Polk, First Lady of James Polk who was President from 1845-1849.

First Lady: My husband and I were always partners. I didn't like all the social affairs and rarely hosted parties. I did insist that gas lights be added to the White House. During the Civil War, the Polk home in Tennessee was was neutral ground.

Calendar: Margaret Smith Taylor, First Lady to Zachary Taylor during his administration, 1849-1850.

First Lady: I spent as much time as possible in the family quarters of the White House. My husband died after 15 months in office. The bands played loud blaring funeral music. That's what I remember - the loud blaring music.

Narrator: Abigail Powers Fillmore, wife and First Lady of Millard Fillmore, President from 1850-1853.

Reporter: When Abigal didn't want to take part in an event, she said her health was poor. She had water pipes and the first bathtub installed in the White House.

Narrator: Jane Pierce was wife of Franklin Pierce, President from 1853-1857. She was sad much of the time. All three of her sons had died - the last one was killed when a coupling on a train broke loose. Her son's head was crushed. She never got over that.

*First Ladies* ☆ **First Ladies** ☆ *First Ladies* ☆

Reporter: Harriet Lane served as First Lady for her uncle and guardian, James Buchanan. When she died, she left most of her estate as an endowment for the Harriet Lane Outpatient Clinic, a home for invalid children. It is still a part of Johns Hopkins Hospital in Baltimore, Maryland.

Calendar: Mary Todd Lincoln, wife and First Lady of Abraham Lincoln, President from 1861-1865.

First Lady: Of all the First Ladies, I am most discussed. I was compulsive and sad. But these were sad times in our country. The Civil War preserved the Union but destroyed many of us - including Abe and me.

Calendar: Eliza McCardle Johnson, First Lady of Andrew Johnson, President from 1865-1869.

First Lady: I was fearful all the while I was in the White House. Lincoln had been assassinated. I was always afraid my Andrew would also be killed. Then they tried to impeach him. My years as First Lady were not happy years.

Calendar: Julia Dent Grant was First Lady of Ulysses S. Grant, President from 1869-1877.

First Lady: I loved being First Lady! My eight years as First Lady were the happiest of my life. Much of the White House was refurbished during those years. It was grand!

Calendar: Lucy Ware Webb Hayes, First Lady of Rutherford B. Hayes, President from 1877-1881.

First Lady: Opportunities for women to vote and to take an active part in society, were increasing. I reflected those times. I was the first First Lady to be college-educated. I advocated temperance and enthusiasm for politics.

*☆ First Ladies ☆ First Ladies ☆ First Ladies ☆*

Calendar: Lucretia Rudolph Garfield, First Lady of James Garfield, President in 1881.

First Lady: I was a teacher by profession. I loved to read the classics and to paint. To my sorrow, my husband was assassinated. After that, I spent the rest of my life collecting and preserving his memories.

Calendar: Frances Folsom Cleveland was First Lady for Grover Cleveland who served as President from 1885-1889 and 1893-1897.

First Lady: I was a White House bride as Grover and I were married after he was president. Grover was 49 and I was 21 when we were married. I enjoyed my work as First Lady.

Calendar: Caroline Scott Harrison was First Lady from 1889-1893, during the presidency of Benjamin Harrison.

First Lady: I liked flowers and had a conservatory built so we could have many flowers at receptions. Orchids were my favorite. I also had the White House wired for electricity. That was a big improvement.

Calendar: Ida Saxton McKinley was First Lady to William McKinley, President from 1897-1901.

First Lady: My mother and three children died within a three-year period of time. I never got over these losses. I also liked the poems of Tennyson and fine laces. I enjoyed playing card games.

Narrator: Edith Kermit Carow Roosevelt was First Lady during the presidency of Theodore Roosevelt from 1901-1909. She was an active First Lady and personally took care of many details. Edith Roosevelt was the first to hire a personal secretary to assist her. This practice continues to this day.

*First Ladies* ☆ **First Ladies** ☆ *First Ladies* ☆

Reporter:      Helen Herron Taft was wife of William Howard
               Taft, president from 1909-1913.  She was one
               of eleven children.  Her nickname was "Nellie."
               She was politically tactful and diplomatic.  One
               of her lasting achievements was co-founding
               the Cincinnati Symphony Orchestra Association.

Narrator:      Ellen Louise Axson Wilson was First Lady when
               Woodrow Wilson was  president from 1913-1914.
               She was of English and Native American ancestors.
               Ellen managed the household, grew vegetables
               and helped her husband and children.  She was
               fluent in German and translated books for Woodrow.
               She served as editor for all of Wilson's writings.
               She died after suffering a bad fall.

Reporter:      Edith Bolling Galt Wilson was the second wife
               of Woodrow Wilson and served as First Lady
               from 1915-1921.  She had musical talent and a
               photographic memory.  She learned to ride a
               bicycle in the basement of the White House.

Narrator:      Florence Mabel Kling DeWolfe Harding was
               First Lady during Warren Harding's administration
               from 1921-1923.  Her nicknames were "Flossie"
               and "the Duchess."  There are unanswered questions
               about how President Harding died.  Florence burned
               all important papers and answered no questions.

Calendar:      Grace Anna Goodhue Coolidge was First Lady
               of President Calvin Coolidge, 1923-1929.

First Lady:    I had been a teacher of the deaf.  Calvin had firm
               ideas about how I should act.  I was not to dance
               in public, drive a car, go horseback riding or
               speak on politics, ride in an airplane, or cut
               my hair short.  He did insist on new and expensive
               clothes for me.  After Cal's death, I traveled more
               and rode in an airplane. I was always a baseball fan.

Calendar:      Lou Henry Hoover was First Lady during the
               presidency of Herbert C. Hoover, 1929-1933.

*First Ladies* ☆ ☆ **First Ladies** ☆ *First Ladies* ☆

First Lady: I was born in Waterloo, Iowa, and was a
well-traveled geology graduate from Stanford.
That's where I met Herbert.  My achievements
include establishing the American Women's
Hospital and the women's division of National
Amateur Athletic Association.  I served as president
of the Girl Scouts and advocated women participating
in politics.  I lived a full life.

Calendar: Anna Eleanor Roosevelt, First Lady of Franklin D.
Roosevelt who was President from 1933-1945.

First Lady: I was active in the women's division of the
Democratic party, the women's Trade Union,
and the League of Women Voters.  One of my
greatest challenges and achievements came when
I chaired the United Nation's commission that
drafted and passed the Declaration of Human Rights.

Calendar: Elizabeth "Bess" Wallace Truman was First Lady
of Harry S. Truman, President from 1945-1953.

First Lady: I was primarily a family woman.  My staff at
the White House liked our family because we
appreciated their efforts.  Harry relied upon me
to know what the public was thinking.  I tempered
his tendency to be impulsive, and to use ill-suited
language in public.  My favorite guest was
Queen Juliana of the Netherlands.

Narrator: Mamie Geneva Doud Eisenhower was First Lady
from 1953-1961, during the presidency of
Dwight "Ike" Eisenhower.  Mamie liked music and
loved to dance. Whenever possible, Mamie
traveled with Ike on his military appointments.
The Eisenhowers were the first to have television
in the White House.  They watched "I Love Lucy"
and other popular shows.

☆ *First Ladies* ☆ **First Ladies** ☆ *First Ladies* ☆

Reporter:     Jacqueline "Jackie" Lee Bouvier Kennedy was
              was the wife of John Kennedy. She served as
              First Lady from 1961-1963.  She was fluent
              in Spanish and French. She was cultured and
              graceful and had the power to charm many people.
              The public was always interested in what she
              did and what clothes she was wearing.

Narrator:     Claudia Alta "Lady Bird" Johnson was Lyndon
              Johnson's wife and First Lady from 1963-1969.
              She was devoted to her family.  When John
              Kennedy was assassinated, "Lady Bird" Johnson
              became First Lady.

Reporter:     Patricia "Pat" Ryan Nixon was First Lady from
              1969-1974.  Her family was always her first concern.
              She was a private person who preferred one-to-one
              contacts rather than huge gatherings and public speeches.

Calendar:     Elizabeth Ann Bloomer Warren Ford was First
              Lady from 1974-1977 when her husband, Gerald
              Ford, was President.

First Lady:   My place in history will probably reflect the more
              serious medical events of my life: breast cancer and
              my battle with drug and alcohol addiction. After these
              troubles, I established the Betty Ford Drug Treatment
              Center.  It is my contribution to those who need help.

Calendar:     Rosalynn Smith Carter was First Lady for
              husband James Earl Carter from 1977-1981.
              She was politically active.

First Lady:   My priority was to improve help to the mentally
              and emotionally handicapped.  I also worked hard
              to support the Equal Rights Amendment.  Jimmy
              and I discussed all matters.  We were a team.
              Some people didn't like that.

*☆ First Ladies ☆* **First Ladies** *☆ First Ladies ☆*

Calendar:     Nancy Robbins Davis Reagan was First Lady
              to Ronald Reagan from 1981-1989.

First Lady:   Certain standards should be maintained at the White
              House.  I reinstated white tie and tails, long formal
              evening gowns, and the wearing of distinctive jewelry
              and entertaining Hollywood celebrities. The cause I
              supported was foster grandparents.

Narrator:     Barbara Bush became First Lady for George Bush
              who was sworn into office in 1989. The public liked
              and trusted her.  She supported reading and literacy
              programs.

              *(This play was written in 1992 when Barbara Bush
              was First Lady.  Update this play to make it current.)*

Reporter:     And who will the next First Lady be?

Narrator:     What cause will she support?

First Lady:   To what degree may I choose my own life,
              and to what degree must I cater to the public's
              image of the First Lady?

Calendar:     Future First Ladies - and First Gentlemen -
              must answer those questions.  Our play is ended.

*The End*

First Ladies ☆ **First Ladies** ☆ *First Ladies* ☆

# *Gandhi*

*Cast*
> *Narrator One (N-1)*
> *Narrator Two (N-2)*
> *Gandhi*
> *Master Teacher*
> *Student One (S-1)*
> *Student Two (S-2)*

*Modifications you may wish to make:*
> *Add more information about Gandhi as well as other information*
> *about India, non-violent approach to problem solving, and political action.*

**N-1:**   How does one begin a play about Mohandas Gandhi -
a man who led India to its independence in 1947?

**N-2:**   How does one begin a play about Mohandas Gandhi -
a political activist who led people by wearing peasant clothes,
spinning cotton, taking salt from the sea, and fasting from food?

**N-1:**   Most stories and plays start at the beginning and
work their way to the end.

**N-2:**   But the story of Gandhi is not like other stories.
The end of the story makes the beginning interesting.

**Teacher:**   The end and the beginning are one. It cannot be divided.

**S-1:**   I cannot read the end and the beginning at
the same time.  That is impossible.

**S-2:**   A life starts, grows, matures, and it ends.  Those are the stages.
Each stage takes time.  One follows after the other.

**Teacher:**   Life is one.  A person is one. A nation is one.

**S-1:**   You say things I don't understand.

**Teacher:**   That is because simple things are often hard to understand.

**S-2:**   Why?

Teacher: Because we clutter our lives with many irrelevant things. This clutter confuses us. It encourages us to fight with each other to gain possession of land, money, position and power.

N-1: This play will attempt to view the life and legacy of Mohandas Gandhi as one. You *(motions to audience)*, come with us, as we review some events that shaped the life and message of Gandhi.

N-2: Come. Let me introduce you to Mr. Gandhi.
*(motions hand to Gandhi)* Ladies and gentlemen, this is Mr. Gandhi.

Gandhi: *(smiles, bows slightly to audience, has hands together in manner of praying).* I am honored to meet you.

S-1: I am honored to meet you, Mr. Gandhi. *(smiles, bows slightly to Gandhi, has hands together in manner of praying).* May I ask you a question?

Gandhi: Certainly. I will answer - if I can.

S-1: How come you wouldn't eat? How come you fasted for many days? Weren't you hungry? People die when they do not eat.

Gandhi: Fasting is a form of speech. In many parts of the Asian world, fasting can achieve what words have not been able to achieve.

S-1: I don't understand that.

Gandhi: Many people do not understand. In India, fasting is an accepted form of religious prayer and political action.

S-2: If I fasted as a means to gain political action, no one would care. Nothing would happen. People will say, "If he (she) wants to fast, who cares? It's his (her) life" And that would be all. Nothing would change.

Gandhi: You would change.

S-2: But nothing else would change. I could just die.

Gandhi:     But your country is not India.  Fasting as a form
of religious conviction and political action _does_
make things happen in India.

N-1:        Mohandas Gandhi was born in Porbandar, India,
on October 2, 1869. He was a shy, serious boy.

N-2:        His father had a quick temper but also a reputation for
fairness and integrity - a sense of right and wrong.

N-1:        His mother was a devout Hindu.  She often fasted.

Gandhi:     My mother was deeply religious.  She would not think
of taking her meals without her daily prayers.

S-1:        Did you and your mother get along?  Did you ever disagree?

Gandhi:     Yes, we got along. And yes, we did disagree.

S-2:        That makes we feel better.  I thought you were always perfect.

Gandhi:     What is perfection?  Perfection and agreeing with
one's mother may not be the same thing.

S-1:        Did you go to school?

Gandhi:     Yes.

S-2:        Were you a good student?

Gandhi:     I had difficulty with the multiplication tables
- that I do remember.  I also remember calling
my teacher names.

S-1:        So you weren't the ideal student?

Gandhi:     No, I was not the ideal student.  My intellect
must have been sluggish.

Teacher:    The environment in which a child's early years are spent
profoundly shapes the adult - make no mistake about that.

N-1:   And so it was with Gandhi.  His early childhood was
       lived in Porbandar in India.  Porbandar is a seaport
       that welcomed ships from many places.

N-2:   A successful seaport or any city - for that matter -
       depends upon an acceptance and tolerance for diversity.

S-1:   What does that mean - "an acceptance and tolerance for diversity?"

S-2:   Does it mean I have to be friends with everyone?

Teacher:  An acceptance and tolerance for diversity means that
          people are allowed to believe whatever beliefs they choose.
          But they also must allow others to make the same choices.

N-1:   In the temple at Porbandar, the readings from the
       Hindu **Bhagavad Gita** and the Muslem **Koran** were
       alternated.  Hinduism and Muslem, along with 20 or
       more other religions, were all accepted in Porbandar.

Gandhi:  For a nonviolent person, the whole world is one family.
         He will thus fear none, nor will others fear him.

Teacher:  Gandhi was lucky to have such a childhood.

S-1:   Mr. Gandhi, I heard that you were married at age 13.
       Is that right?

Gandhi:  Yes. It was the custom for us to be married at that age.

S-2:   Did you know your wife?  Was she pretty?  Did you like her?

Gandhi:  So many questions!  The answer is one: yes.

N-1:   His wife was the daughter of a Porbandar merchant.
       She had no schooling and had lived comfortably.

N-2:   They were a good and happy couple.  Kasturba, his wife,
       was Gandhi's wife, partner, and loyal follower.

Teacher:  They lived a simple life.  Gandhi thought it was wrong to
          kill animals for food or to use their hides.

S-2:        You were a small man.  Did that bother you?

Gandhi:     Bother me?  Why would my size bother me?

S-2:        Lots of men think they have to be big and strong.

Gandhi:     Strength does not come from physical capacity.
            Strength comes from strong will power and determination.

S-1:        What did you do for a living?

Gandhi:     I was a lawyer - in South Africa and in India.

S-2:        You spent a lot of time in prison.
            Why were you arrested so many times?

Gandhi:     It is honorable to spend time in prison for a just cause.

S-2:        Why were you arrested so many times?

Gandhi:     The British did not agree with many of my actions or attitudes.
            India was under the rule of the British.  There were certain
            things we could not do, and certain things we had to do.

S-1:        Like what?

Gandhi:     We had to buy salt from England.  Salt, as you know, is
            essential for life.  It was a crime if you made your own salt
            or bought it from anyone other than England.

S-2:        What did you do?

Gandhi:     I encouraged our people to make their own salt.

S-1:        How do you make salt?

Gandhi:     Some seas and all oceans are salty.  You make salt by
            getting rid of the water.  After the water is gone, the
            salt remains.  It is not a complicated process.

S-2:        Did the British care that you were making your own salt?

Gandhi:     Yes. They saw it as a protest against their laws.

S-1:     It was a protest, wasn't it?

Gandhi:  Yes.  It was a nonviolent protest.

S-2:     How can a protest be nonviolent?

Gandhi:  Some people protest through violence.  Then many
         people are killed.  Killing people does not change
         attitudes and minds.  You must find a way to change
         laws and attitudes without killing people.

S-1:     How did you discover that nonviolence could win?

Gandhi:  I did not discover it.  Truth and nonviolence are
         as old as the hills.

N-1:     Gandhi's life was very busy.  He kept to a schedule.
         He was punctual and expected others to be the same.

N-2:     His day began early in the morning - around 3:00 or 4:00 a.m.
         He liked the cool quiet Indian morning for meditation.
         From these early morning meditations came renewal
         of spirit and physical energy.

Teacher: The Indian people gave Gandhi the title "Mahatma"  - which
         means "great soul."  Mahatma Gandhi was a great soul
         because his entire life was spent seeking truth.

N-1:     Gandhi believed truth could be known only through
         tolerance and concern for every person.

N-2:     He overcame fear himself and taught others to master fear.
         His notion of nonviolence was one of courage and action.

S-1:     Nonviolence may also reflect a fear of confronting people.

N-1:     That is not the case with Gandhi.  He never backed down from
         a cause that he thought right and just.  He never initiated violence
         nor approved of physical violence.

Gandhi:  It is honorable to spend time in prison for a just cause.

S-2:    Why is Gandhi often pictured spinning cotton?

Teacher:    Gandhi was the father of modern India. Spinning cotton and weaving it into cloth showed that India could be economically independent, and that there was dignity in common labor.

Gandhi:    Spinning cotton thread and weaving our own cloth was a nonviolent way of showing that we could provide our own clothes. We did not require the British textile industry.

Teacher:    The efforts with the cotton cloth and salt raised the pride of all India. Personal and national pride pave the way for a country's independence.

N-1:    India gained its independence in 1947. Much violence did occur but Gandhi would denounce it and fast to stop the bloodshed.

N-2:    He gave speeches and held meetings so that India could be a free and united nation. India was given independence - or home rule, as it is called.

N-1:    In 1948, Mahatma Gandhi was assassinated by a man who feared Gandhi's program of tolerance for all creeds and religions.

N-2:    His story is one of courage in the face of great political power struggles.

N-1:    He combined the genius of a politician and the fervor of a religious leader with the incessant search for truth.

Teacher:    The beginning and the end of this story are one. Thank you, Mr. Mahatma Mohandas Gandhi.

*The End*

# Robert E. Lee

*Cast*
> *Historian*
> *Robert E. Lee*
> *Narrator*
> *Spirit of the South*

*Modifications you may wish to make:*
> *Display books on the Civil War and Robert E. Lee.*

South:   The South is a gracious, hospitable place
- for those who appreciate it and value it.

Narrator:   Robert E. Lee readily accepted loyalty
to the South.  It was his home and heritage.

Historian:   The time is 1807 -  January 19, 1807. Lee is
born in Westmoreland County, Virginia. His
parents are Henry and Ann Lee.

Lee:   One of my early remembrances is of my father
and his admiration for George Washington.

Narrator:   When Lee was a child of 11, his father died
and his mother became ill.  Lee took care
of his mother and went to school.

Historian:   Robert E. Lee went to West Point Military Academy
from 1825 to 1829.  He was a good student.

Lee:   At West Point, I studied math, science, drawing, and
other general studies.  We marched every day.

Narrator:   Lee married Mary Custis in 1831.
He and his wife had seven children.

South: Robert E. Lee was one of our finest sons.
He loved the Nation. He loved the South. He
did what was expected of him. He did his duty.

Lee: My life was filled with my family and duty to my
country. I fought in the Mexican War. Then
I could return to my beloved family and the South.

Historian: Lee was a leader. He understood governments,
personal honor, military strategies, and education.
Using this understanding, he served as superintendent
to West Point Military Academy from 1852-1855.

Narrator: But the Civil War invaded the lives of many people.
It exploded upon the nation in 1861. The North was
fighting the South. Lincoln had declared war to
preserve the union.

Lee: What was I to do? I did not believe in slavery.
Nor did I believe in fighting my own relatives
and the South. In a Civil War, you cannot be
neutral. You have to choose one side.

Historian: Lee resigned his Union Army commission and became
the leader of the southern Confederate forces.

Narrator: At first, the South won many battles.
Then the North began to win.

Historian: The North had more factories and soldiers. But the
South had better generals - particularly Robert E. Lee.

South: Most of the battles were fought on southern soil.
Many of our cities and most of our fields lay
in ruin. Our crops were destroyed and no new
ones could be planted.

Historian: Plants and animals were destroyed by battles and fires.

| | |
|---|---|
| <u>Lee</u>: | Thousands of our people died and were wounded. If the War continued, the South would have nothing. |
| <u>Narrator</u>: | Both sides lost heavily. Many died. Many more were wounded. |
| <u>Lee</u>: | The South could hold out no longer. We had no food and no supplies. Civilians and military were dying by the thousands. To preserve the South, we had to surrender. My generals agreed. |
| <u>Historian</u>: | Lee surrendered to Grant on April 9, 1865. The battles stopped. Technically, the Civil War was over. |
| <u>South</u>: | The entire nation bears the emotional scars of a country that warred against itself. The wounds were inflicted from 1861-1865. The healing continues. |
| <u>Lee</u>: | After the war, I did all I could to build up tolerance among people - all people. |
| <u>Historian</u>: | Robert E. Lee, a man of integrity, self-discipline, and honor, died October 12, 1870, in Lexington, Virginia. |
| <u>South</u>: | Robert E. Lee was one the South's finest. We shared him with the nation. |

*The End*

# Abraham Lincoln

*Cast*
> Lincoln
> Historian One
> Historian Two
> Historian Three
> Chorus - represents the public
> Narrator

## Modifications you may wish to make:
Add other quotations or points of interest on Lincoln
that you consider appropriate to the reading.

| | |
|---|---|
| Narrator: | Ladies and gentlemen (girls and boys).  The subject of our Readers' Theater play is Abraham Lincoln. |
| Historian One: | When polls are taken to determine who is the most popular United States president, Abraham Lincoln is usually choice Number One. |
| Chorus: | We, the general public, like Abraham Lincoln. He was like us.  He was a man we understood. |
| Historian Two: | Lincoln was born in a log cabin near Hodgenville, Kentucky, in 1809. |
| Narrator: | He held books and reading in great esteem. |
| Lincoln: | "It is of no consequence to be in a large town... The books, and your capacity for understanding them, are just the same in all places."* |
| Historian One: | 1816. |
| Historian Three: | In 1816, Abraham Lincolns' family moves from Kentucky to southwest Indiana. |
| Historian One: | 1818. |
| Historian Two: | In 1818, Nancy Hanks Lincoln, Abe's mother, dies. |

| | |
|---|---|
| Historian One: | 1830. |
| Historian Three: | Abe moves to New Salem, Illinois. |
| Historian One: | 1832. |
| Historian Two: | Abe becomes a captain in the Black Hawk War. |
| Historian One: | 1834. |
| Historian Three: | Elected to the Illinois State Legislature. |
| Chorus: | We, the public, trusted Lincoln. He came from a humble background. |
| Lincoln: | "There is both a power and a magic in popular opinion."** |
| Historian One: | 1836. |
| Historian Two: | Lincoln begins law practice. |
| Lincoln: | "We know nothing of what will happen in the future, but by the analogy of past experience."√ |
| Historian One: | 1842. |
| Historian Three: | Abraham Lincoln marries Mary Todd. |
| Historian One: | 1847 - 1849. |
| Historian Two: | Lincoln serves in the U.S. House of Representatives. |
| Narrator: | Abraham Lincoln was well-known in Illinois. He became known to the nation through the Lincoln-Douglas debates in 1858. |
| Lincoln: | I liked the debates. They gave me a chance to express many ideas. |

| | |
|---|---|
| Narrator: | After the Lincoln-Douglas debates, the general public wanted Abraham Lincoln to run for president. |
| Chorus: | We want Lincoln! We want Lincoln! |
| Historian One: | Lincoln was against slavery. |
| Lincoln: | "As I would not be a slave, so I would not be a master." √√ |
| Historian Two: | Lincoln believed that slavery could destroy this nation. In his "house-divided" speech he said: |
| Lincoln: | "A house divided against itself cannot stand. I believe this government cannot endure, permanently half slave and half free." |
| Historian Three: | Lincoln said those words when he accepted the Republican nomination for the Senate in 1858. This statement clearly said that Lincoln was against slavery because slavery could destroy the nation. |
| Narrator: | 1860. |
| Historian One: | Lincoln is elected President. South Carolina secedes from the union. |
| Narrator: | 1861. |
| Historian Two: | Abraham Lincoln is inaugurated as the 16th President of the United States. Fort Sumter falls and the Civil War begins. |
| Chorus: | We are at war! We are at war! Our country is fighting itself. We are at war! |
| Narrator: | 1862. |
| Historian Three: | Lincoln calls for 300,000 men to enlist for three years. |
| Narrator: | Civil war - a country fighting itself - is a terrible thing. No one truly wins a civil war because everyone loses family, resources and dignity. |

| | |
|---|---|
| Historian One: | Lincoln was a melancholy man - that means he was a man given to deep thoughts and intense sorrow. He puzzled and worried what to do. |
| Historian Two: | He looked to history for solutions. But he found no answers there. |
| Lincoln: | "The solutions of the past are inadequate for the stormy present. As our case is new, so must we think anew and act anew. *** |
| Narrator: | 1863. |
| Historian Three: | Lincoln issues the Emancipation Proclamation declaring freedom for slaves. |
| Historian One: | It was also in 1863 that Lincoln gave the speech that is most quoted: "The Gettysburg Address." |
| Lincoln: | "Fourscore and seven years ago, our fathers brought forth on this continent a new nation, conceived in liberty and dedicated to the proposition that all men are created equal." |
| Chorus: | Our country is falling apart! Our country is falling apart! |
| Narrator: | 1864. |
| Historian Two: | Lincoln is re-elected president. Andrew Johnson is vice-president. |
| Narrator: | 1865. |
| Historian Three: | The Confederate capitol of Richmond falls. |
| Historian One: | General Robert E. Lee surrenders to Ulysses S. Grant at Appomattox courthouse. |
| Chorus: | The war is over! The war is over! |

| | |
|---|---|
| Historian Two: | John Wilkes Booth shoots Lincoln in Washington, D.C. He dies on April 15, 1865. |
| Chorus: | Our president is dead!  Who will take care of us? Our president is dead!  Our president is dead! |
| Narrator: | Lincoln was not the first government leader to be assassinated, nor will he be the last.  But in the history of the United States, the loss of Lincoln at this point in history was a loss beyond measure. |
| Historian One: | When a person dies, the facts of his life are fixed - no more facts are added.  What does change is the interpretation of those facts. |
| Historian Two: | In the case of Lincoln, there was a dramatic change in public sentiment. During his life - particularly during the Civil War - he was loved and hated, praised and condemned. |
| Historian Three: | But when he died, the public became more tolerant of Lincoln's views. |
| Chorus: | We didn't always like Lincoln, but now he's dead. People shouldn't kill presidents.  It's not right. Now we think he's a hero. |
| Historian One: | And so he was. |
| Historian Two: | He helped save a nation. |
| Historian Three: | He died for that cause. |
| Chorus: | Rest in peace, Mr. Abraham Lincoln. Rest in peace. |

*The End*

Quotations used in this play:
* Letter to I. Reavis, November 5, 1855.
**The "Lost" Speech at Bloomington, May 29, 1856.
√ Speech on Subtreasury, December 20, 1839.
√√ Letter written in 1858.
*** Annual message to Congress, December 1, 1862.

Vol. Two - **62**

Readers' Theater. MEN WHO SUPPORTED CAUSES page 1

# Men Who Supported Causes

*Cast*
*Reporter*
*Cesar Chavez*
*Father Flanagan*
*Albert Schweitzer*
_____ *add names - if you added information* ( *see last page of play*)


*Modifications you may wish to make:*
*List on cards the names of the men and the causes each supported.*
Cesar Chavez - migrant workers
Father Flanagan - home for boys
Albert Schweitzer - medical help and world peace
_____ *add names - if you added information* (*see last page of play*)


**Reporter:** Welcome to our theater.  Our guests today are
Cesar Chavez, Father Flanagan, and Albert Schweitzer.
( *add names - if you added information - see last page of play*)
Each will introduce himself.

**Chavez:** I am Cesar Chavez. My cause was my people -
the migrant workers.

**Flanagan:** I am Father Flanagan, founder of Boys Town
- a place in Nebraska where young people
can get a new start in life.

**Schweitzer:** I am Albert Schweitzer, medical doctor in Africa
and promoter of peace throughout the world.

_____ *(Add names - if you added information - see last page of play)*


**Reporter:** Thank you, gentlemen, for being with us today.
Mr. Chavez, the first question is directed to you.
You supported the cause of migrant workers.  Why?

**Chavez:** My family had an 80-acre farm in Yuma, Arizona. We raised animals, grains, and vegetables. My father also ran a country store. We lost all this because my father had been tricked in a bad business deal.

**Reporter:** You then went to California and became a migrant worker. Exactly who is a migrant worker and what does a migrant worker do?

**Chavez:** A migrant worker is one who travels from place to place when different vegetables, grains, or fruits are ready to be harvested. We traveled a lot, but our families were together. Our schooling was interrupted.

**Reporter:** Many migrant children did not progress past 6th grade. You graduated from 8th grade and worked in the fields full time. Will you comment on this?

**Chavez:** By the time I graduated from 8th grade, I had been in 36 schools. I kept working in the fields and moving from school to school. I kept studying. It wasn't easy.

**Reporter:** You became an activist for the cause of migrant workers. What opportunities did you want for the migrants?

**Chavez:** Many migrant workers are Mexican-Americans - my people. I wanted better and safer working conditions. We also needed better food, housing, medical and legal aid.

**Reporter:** Those are major causes. With your leadership, the National Farm Workers Association was founded in Fresno, California, in 1962. It became known as "La Causa". What does "La Causa" mean?

**Chavez:** "La Causa" is Spanish for "The Cause." The cause is defined as the struggle for human rights and dignity for migrant and farm workers.

**Reporter:** You made enemies.

*Vol. Two -* **64**

Readers' Theater. MEN WHO SUPPORTED CAUSES page 3

Chavez: I did not want to make enemies. But people who paid low wages, offered unsafe working conditions, and gave little medical and legal help saw me as the enemy.

Reporter: How did La Causa move forward?

Chavez: La Causa moved forward through lectures, economic boycotts, and the courage of many people.

Reporter: La Causa continues. Thank you Mr. Chavez. *(slight pause)* Our next guest is Father Flanagan, a Roman Catholic priest. Father Flanagan, why did you start Boys Town?

Flanagan: I started Boys Town - near Omaha, Nebraska - in 1917. I believed that if boys were given the best possible home, education, and training, they would grow up to be useful adults.

Reporter: When you first borrowed $90 to rent an old house in Omaha to care for five boys, did you know you would devote the rest of your life to helping boys?

Flanagan: No. My initial purpose was to help those five boys. From this beginnin, came Boys Town - a private institution for homeless and underprivileged boys of every race and religion.

Reporter: What opportunities were offered to the boys?

Flanagan: The boys were given housing and schooling - including technical or vocational training. This training was needed so that they could support themselves and contribute to society.

Reporter: Father Flanagan, is there any other information you'd like to give to us today?

Flanagan: Yes. Boys Town now serves boys and girls. It also operates as a research center for the study of youth development, and an institute for children with communication disorders.

Readers' Theater. MEN WHO SUPPORTED CAUSES page 4

*Vol. Two --* **65**

Reporter:     Thank you for being with us today.

Flanagan:     I was happy to be here. Come visit Boys Town,
              west of Omaha, Nebraska. We welcome visitors.

Reporter:     Our next guest is Albert Schweitzer. Dr. Schweitzer
              is a physician, philosopher, organist, and theologian.
              Welcome, Dr. Schweitzer.

Schweitzer:   Thank you for inviting me.

Reporter:     You were an accomplished musician who
              could fill concert halls with the works of Bach.
              Why did you give up that career to become a
              doctor - a doctor in Africa?

Schweitzer:   I had many interests and many talents. In
              addition to being a musician, I was also a
              philosopher, theologian, and historian.
              But there was still a void inside of me.

Reporter:     You turned to medicine and Africa. Why?

Schweitzer:   In medicine, I could give immediate help. And
              people of Africa needed me. We made a good match.

Reporter:     Your medical work was with the needy in small
              villages - not in large city hospitals. Why?

Schweitzer:   As I said, I needed to be needed. The African
              people in the villages needed me.

Reporter:     In your later years, you promoted the cause
              of peace. Why and how did you do that?

Schweitzer:   I feared a nuclear war would destroy our world.
              I did what I could do. I wrote letters to rulers
              of countries. I gave speeches to anyone who
              would listen to me.

Reporter:     Some people listened.  We will listen.
              What is your message to us today?

Schweitzer:   I urge every person here today to make a contribution
              to the world.  A contribution to the world is something
              that improves the world today and will live on.

Reporter:     Thank you, Dr. Albert Schweitzer.

---

*---- optional insert ---*

*Add other information about people who supported causes.*
*Format: the reporter introduces and asks the first question.*
*The person responds.  There may be one or several*
*lines of dialogue.*

*If you add information here, add introductions to the*
*opening lines also.*

---

Reporter:     Our guests today have been men who supported
              causes. Perhaps in years to come, your name and the
              cause you supported will be included in this play.

Chavez:       Each of us responded to a need of our time.

Flanagan:     We served people who were not able - at the
              moment - to help themselves.

Schweitzer:   Our contributions gave our lives a sense of
              fulfillment.  And in so doing we helped others.

Reporter:     Thank you for being with us today.
              *(to audience)* Our play is ended.

*The End*

# Named After People

*Cast*

> *Narrator*
> *Lexicographer One*
> *Lexicographer Two*
> *Student*

*Modifications you may wish to make:*
> *Add other words that come from proper names.*
> *Use word cards to show the words and their meaning.*
> *Words based on name, used in this play are:*

| | | | | |
|---|---|---|---|---|
| ampere | boycott | Braille | chauvinism | graham crackers |
| magnolia | maverick | mesmerize | ohm | poinsettia |
| sandwich | teddy bear | watt | volt | |

**Narrator:** The topic of this play is words.

**One:** There are words in the English language that are based on peoples' names.

**Two:** The word is created deliberately or it gradually comes into usage.

**Student:** Can you give me some examples of words based on peoples' names?

**One:** From the world of electricity, we have four such words: ampere, ohm, watt, and volt.

**Two:** Ampere is a unit for measuring electricity. It is named after Andre' Ampere, a French physicist.

**One:** Ohm is a measure of electrical resistance and is named after Georg Simon Ohm.

**Two:** A watt and volt are measures of electrical power. They are named after Alessandro Volta and James Watt.

Student:  My friend reads books in Braille. Braille is a
series of raised dots and dashes that represent
letters. She reads with her fingertips.

One:  Louis Braille was a Frenchman who became blind when
he was a little boy. He learned the alphabet by feeling the
shape of twigs shaped into letters. Braille wanted to learn
more and reading by feeling twigs took too long.

Two:  He heard about a French Army captain who was
experimenting with raised dots. Braille refined
the system of raised letters. His name remains.

Narrator:  The word "chauvinism" is used today. A chauvinist
is someone who is loyal without judging the person
or cause to which loyalty is given.

One:  "Chauvinism" is named after Nicholas Chauvin,
a soldier who worshipped France and Napolean
uncritically.

Narrator:  To "boycott" something means to refuse to do business
with someone. The word comes from the name of
Charles Boycott, a British army officer.

Two:  Charles Boycott was the namer and first victim of
a boycott. He raised land rents. The tenants refused
to pay the additional taxes. Local merchants refused
to do business with him. And the word boycott has
been in our language since 1880.

Narrator:  The magnolia tree was named after Pierre Magnol,
professor of botany in Montpelier, France.

Two:  The poinsettia is named after Joel Poinsett,
a native of South Carolina, who brought back
the large showy flowers from Mexico.

Student:  There are always graham crackers in our house.
They are named after Sylvester Graham, an
American vegetarian reformer in dietetics.

One:    A maverick is someone who doesn't follow the rules
        or cannot be controlled. Samuel Maverick, a Texan
        who didn't brand his cattle, gave us the word.

Two:    To mesmerize someone is to hold them under
        your power.  Friedrich Mesmer, an Austrian
        physician who practiced hypnotism, gave us the word.

Student:    I eat sandwiches. Peanut butter and jelly is my favorite.
            John Montagu, fourth Earl of Sandwich, invented the
            sandwich so he could gamble without stopping for a meal.

Narrator:    Do you have a teddy bear?  Theodore "Teddy"
             Roosevelt, president of the United States,  spared
             the life of a bear cub on a hunting trip in Mississippi.
             The teddy bear is named from this incident.

One:    These and many other words in our language are based
        on the people who invented, discovered or started something.

Two:    When the dictionaries are rewritten, will there
        be a word that is based on your name?

Student:    There might be.

---

--- Optional Insert:

Create an object, an attitude, or a process, and name it after yourselves.
Report it in this format:

*"My name is* _____. *The word based on*

*my name is* _____ (say the word) *because  I*

(list the object/attitude/process developed)_____

_____.

---

Narrator:    Our play is ended.  See you in the dictionary.

*The End*

# People Associated with Religions

*Cast*
> *Narrator*
> *Historian*
> *Believer*

*Modifications you may wish to make.*
> *Add information on religions that are not represented here.*
> *Discuss the fact that some religions are not associated with specific*
>       *persons, but rather with specific beliefs.*
> *Reassign lines to accommodate more readers.*
>
> *If you wish, change lines in the play to represent your beliefs.*

Historian: Many people are part of a religious group.
 These groups are alike in some ways.
 In other ways, they are different.

Narrator: We will review persons who are associated
 with religions.

Believer: I represent the "believer" - that person who
 ascribes to the religion under review.

Historian: If the religion to which you belong is not
 listed here, there will be the opportunity
 for you to add that information.

Narrator: Buddha is associated with the Buddhist religion.
 Buddha was a prince in India several hundred
 years B.C.. After years of thinking about life,
 he taught self-denial and universal brotherhood.

Believer: Buddhism stresses physical and spiritual discipline.
 The goal is to attain <u>Nirvana</u> - a state of complete peace.

Narrator: John Calvin is the founder of Calvinism.

Believer: Calvinism stressed that people are saved through
 God's grace - not through individual efforts.

**Historian:** Christianity is based on the teachings of Jesus Christ. Jesus lived during the days of the Roman Empire.

**Believer:** Christians believe that Christ died so that we could be saved.

**Narrator:** Mary Baker Eddy was an American religious reformer. She is the founder of Christian Science.

**Believer:** Christian Scientists believe that illness can be conquered through spiritual power. They choose not to be treated by medical doctors for their illness.

**Historian:** The Jewish faith is also called Judaism. Abraham is considered its founder.

**Believer:** Jews believe there is one God. Their faith is based on the teachings of the Torah - the first five books of the Bible.

**Narrator:** Martin Luther is the founder of the Lutheran religion.

**Believer:** Lutherans believe that faith saves people.

**Historian:** Joseph Smith is the founder of Mormonism.

**Believer:** Mormons believe that God's revelations have occurred and continue to occur.

**Narrator:** John Wesley was an English clergyman who founded the Methodist religion.

**Believer:** Methodists believe that we have social responsibilities. Doctrines and organizations change, but obligations towards each other and society remain constant.

**Historian:** Mohammed is the founder of Islam - the Muslem religion. Moslems believe that there is one God, Allah, and that Mohammed was Allah's prophet.

**Believer:** As a devout Muslim, I pray five times a day. I fast during month of Ramadan. I do not eat pork or drink alcohol. I make gifts to the poor. A pilgrimage to the holy city of Mecca will be my life's goal.

---

*--- optional insert---*

*Readers and / or audience may add the names of persons associated with a religion. One basic tenet, belief, or practice of that religion should be reviewed.*

*---optional insert ---*

*Include information on religions that are not associated with a specific person. These could include, but are not limited to, Hinduism, Unitarianism, Taoism ,...*

---

**Narrator:** Religions, and the beliefs that flow from them, have played a part in the history of the world. They will continue to do so.

**Believer:** Let us respect the beliefs of others.

**Historian:** Our play is ended.

*The End.*

# People Who Improved Communications

*Cast*

> *Bell, Alexander*
> *Braille, Louis*
> *Champollion, Jean Francois*
> *Gregg, John Robert*
> *Marconi, Guglielmo*
> *Sign Language Representative*
> *Historian*
> *Consumer*

*Modifications you may wish to make:*
> *Add other information on people who improved communications*
> *that will be of interest to participants in this readers theater play.*

**Consumer:** Communications surround us every minute of every day. Our Readers' Theater today will talk about people who improved communications.

**Historian:** Many people contributed improvements. Mr. John Robert Gregg is our first guest.

**Gregg:** Hello. My name is John Robert Gregg. I was born in Ireland. I invented the Gregg method of shorthand.

**Historian:** Shorthand is a fast way of writing. With shorthand, you can write almost as fast as a person can talk.

**Consumer:** How is that possible?

**Gregg:** My method of shorthand developed certain symbols for combined vowel sounds. You write only those consonants that you hear.

**Historian:** Several others developed shorthand methods but Gregg's is the mostly widely used method.

**Consumer:** I learned shorthand at business school. Because I know shorthand, my pay is higher than some of the other secretaries'.

**Gregg:**    It is a useful skill for employment and personal life.

**Historian:**    Thank you, Mr. Gregg.  Our next guest represents all people who developed and use sign language - a system of hand signals and gestures to represent letters and words

**Sign:**    On behalf of all developers and users of sign language, I thank you for inviting me to be one of your guests.

**Consumer:**    Who first developed sign language?

**Sign:**    The Abbe de l'Epee founded the first school for the deaf in Paris, France,  in 1760.  He used sign language to spell words.  Other people added to this methodology.

**Historian:**    Sign language was used by South American Indians. It was also used by religious monks who took a vow of silence - that is, they promised never to talk.

**Sign:**    Sign language is also used in sports to call or report judgments made by officials.

**Consumer:**    Many people develop personal hand movements to indicate messages that all understand or only a few understand.

**Historian:**    Thank you for that information.  Our next guest is the French scholar, Jean Francois Champollion.  He translated the information on the Egyptian Rosetta Stone.

**Champollion:** The Rosetta Stone was uncovered by Napoleon's engineers in 1799.  It was found in the mud of the Nile River near Rosetta, Egypt.

**Historian:**    Before the Rosetta Stone was translated, no one knew what the Egyptian hieroglyphics - writings - meant.  The Rosetta Stone provided the basic information on the Egyptian language.

Champollion: The Rosetta Stone was written in three languages. You could tell it was three languages because each of the three sections looked different.

Consumer: How did you figure out that the message said the same things - said it in three different languages?

Champollion: First I translated the Greek portion. Using the Greek portion as a guide, I picked out the same proper names in the Egyptian texts.

Historian: With the proper nouns identified, he progressed through the other words by an analysis of writing patterns, and by comparisons with the ancient Coptic and modern Egyptian language.

Champollion: When the Rosetta Stone was completely translated, it was revealed that the same message was written in three different languages. Using the Stone as a dictionary, other ancient Egyptian writings could be translated.

Consumer: Thank you, Jean Francois Champollion. We appreciate your major contribution to the field of communications.

Historian: Without your help, much of the ancient Egyptian world would be unknown to us.

Consumer: Are there other people who unlocked languages?

Historian: In the 1970s, Mitchel DaHood unlocked the meaning of Ugarit writings, a language of the ancient kingdom of Urartu located in the Middle East.

Consumer: Any other person?

Historian: Yes. Sequoya invented a system of writing that could record the Native American Cherokee language. His chief aim was to record the tribal culture of his people.

**Consumer:**    We are grateful to DaHood, Sequoya, and all other persons who recorded and translated histories of people.

**Historian:**    Our next three guests are probably known to most of you.  They are Alexander Graham Bell, Guglielmo Marconi, and Louis Braille. Each will introduce himself and tell his contribution.

**Braille:**    I am Louis Braille.  I was a 15-year-old blind French student who developed the system of raised dot for reading.  A blind person could read by feeling the raised dots on the pages.

**Consumer:**    What a great idea! Can you write messages in Braille?

**Braille:**    Yes. We write Braille with a special instrument that raises dots on the paper but does not poke through it.

**Bell:**    I am Alexander Graham Bell.  I invented the telephone. I imagine every person in this audience uses my invention.

**Consumer:**    It would be hard to imagine a world without a phone to call 911, request information, and talk with friends - for hours and hours.

**Bell:**    Ah, yes - phone conversations that last for hours and hours.  Those are not what I had in mind when I invented the telephone.

**Historian:**    You were only 27 when you developed the principle of sending speech electrically.  How old were you when you patented the telephone?

**Bell:**    I was 29 years old in 1876 - the year my telephone was patented. I continued to create in my remaining 45 years.  My associates and I developed wax discs for phonograph records.

**Historian:**    His other achievements include a device which helped breathing, a method of locating icebergs by detecting echoes from them, and a process of making fresh water from vapor in the air.

**Bell:**  I was also interested in man-lifting kites and spent considerable time and energy on those experiments. As I grew older, I spent a lot of time in my laboratory and at my piano - playing Scottish tunes. But I have talked enough. It is Marconi's turn to speak.

**Marconi:**  I am Guglielmo Marconi. As my name suggests, I am of Italian birth and very proud of it. It was in 1894 that I read a newspaper article about magnetic waves of electricity that traveled through space. With that basic information I developed a system of radio waves - wireless telegraphy.

**Historian:**  The British military was interested in wireless telegraphy. In 1899, Marconi successfully sent a message - without wires - across the English Channel. In 1901, he successfully sent the message across the Atlantic Ocean.

**Marconi:**  Messages sent by wireless telegraphy were here to stay. From that point on, radio, as we know it today, was possible. The first United States commercial radio station opened in Pittsburgh, Pennsylvania, in 1920.

**Consumer:**  Thanks to all of you for your improvements in communications.

**Historian:**  This concludes our play today.

*The End*

# Psychologists

*Cast*

*Psychologist*
*Client*
*Sigmund Freud*
*Carl Jung*
*Williams James*
*Ivan Pavlov*
*B.F. Skinner*
*Karen Horney*
*Harry Harlow*
*Abraham Maslow*
*Lewis Terman*

*Modifications you may wish to make:*
*Add more psychologists may be added.*
*Invite local psychologists as guests of honor.*

| | |
|---|---|
| Psychologist: | Psychology is the study of our minds and how they work. |
| Client: | Does my mind work the same as the mind of other people? |
| Psychologist: | The biological system through which our minds operate seems to be the same, or nearly the same, for all people. |
| Client: | But I don't respond to things the way others do. If we process information the same way, why don't we react the same way? |
| Psychologist: | Good question. We are influenced by genetic factors, and the attitudes of those around us. Our psychologists in this play will introduce themselves. They will say their names and the contributions they made to the field of psychology. |

Sigmund Freud:   I am Sigmund Freud. People may not agree with me but they all know what I achieved. I developed psychoanalysis. I helped to establish the fields psychology and psychiatry.

Karen Horney:   I am Karen Horney, a psychologist who dared to differ with Sigmund Freud. Freud said that women felt inferior to men and that they were inferior. I contended that many women felt that way - not because women were inferior to men - but because society told them they were inferior.

Carl Jung:   My name is Carl Jung. I believed that people can be classified into two major groups: <u>introverts</u> and <u>extroverts</u>

Client:   What is the difference?

Carl Jung:   Introverts enjoy time alone. Extroverts prefer the company of others.

Client:   Is there a way people are all alike?

Carl Jung:   I believed that all human beings share a collective unconsciousness. This means that all people have the same basic human needs.

Williams James:   I am William James. I was both a philosopher and a psychologist. I was one of the first to suggest that people have instincts. Instincts help us survive because we don't have to learn them. We can just use them.

B.F. Skinner:   My name is B.F. Skinner. I believed that humans and animals learned in the same way. I said that all learning is done through a conditioned reflex.

Client:   Please explain a conditioned or learned reflex.

B.F. Skinner:   If I am rewarded, I continue an action. I discontinue an action if I am punished or not rewarded. Our life is a collection of learned conditioned responses and reflexes.

| | |
|---|---|
| Ivan Pavlov: | I am Ivan Pavlov. My research agreed with Skinner's work. You will often see reference to "Pavlov's dogs." This refers to the dogs which formed saliva at the sound of the bell. |
| Client: | What did the bell mean? |
| Ivan Pavlov: | The dogs had learned that the bell preceded the arrival of food. Even when I discontinued feeding them at the sound of the bell, the dogs continued to salivate at the bell's sound. |
| Harry Harlow: | My name is Harry Harlow. I studied developmental stages and social behavior through observing various species of monkeys. I showed that close human love at an early age is necessary if an infant is to grow up normal and healthy. |
| Abraham Maslow: | My name is Abraham Maslow. I am honored to be called the founder of Humanistic Psychology. |
| Client: | What do Humanists believe? |
| Abraham Maslow: | Humanists believe that individuals control their own values and choices. We are not entirely controlled by our genetics and environment. |
| Lewis Terman: | I am Lewis Terman. Gifted bright children were of particular interest to me. I studied 1500 bright children. I also revised intelligence tests for use with English-speaking students. |
| Client: | I can see that psychologists have different specialities and different points of view. How can they be good psychologists if they do not agree on basic viewpoints? |
| Psychologist: | Psychologists are similar to parents and teachers. We all know that we want the best for those in our care. But we each meet the needs we see in different ways. |

Client:   So you can have a favorite psychologist, just
          as you can have a favorite teacher. Is that right?

Psychologist:   Yes.

Client:   How do I know if I need the help of a psychologist?

Psychologist:   We offer help to those who find life too demanding
                because of recent or prolonged circumstances that
                are difficult to bear. If you need help, all psychologists
                may not be equally suited for your needs.

Client:   How can I tell if one is good for me?

Psychologist:   You'll know after the first or second visit.
                Feel free to go to another psychologist if
                one does not meet your needs.

Client:   Thanks for this information.

Psychologists:   You're welcome.  Our play is ended.


*The End*

# Storytellers

*Cast*
> *Storyteller One*
> *Storyteller Two*
> *Mother Goose*
> *Aesop*
> *Reading Authority*

*Modifications you may wish to make:*
> *Add information from other Mother Goose rhymes*
> *and Aesop's fables.*

**Goose:** There is no proof that I, Mother Goose, ever existed. I am noted for stories and rhymes to be read or told to children.

**Authority:** Upon that fact everyone agrees.

**Two:** One version says that Mother Goose was really Elizabeth Vergoose - a woman of Boston, Massachusetts. Her son-in-law published the songs and rhymes she sang to her grandchildren. This cannot be proven since no copy of the book can be found.

**One:** Another version claims Mother Goose is a direct translation from the French **Mere l'Oye**. In 1697, Charles Perrault published the first book in which Mother Goose was used. It contains stories but no rhymes.

**Authority:** Perrault did not make up these stories but rather collected them from storytellers.

**Goose:** You can talk all you want. I know I am the one who made up rhymes and jingles that have delighted children for years.

**Authority:** The rhythm and flow of language in Mother Goose help very young children to understand how language sounds and how it is used to communicate.

Two:     In 1760, John Newbery, the first English publisher
         of children's books, brought out a tiny book illustrated
         with woodcuts. The book contained 52 rhymes and
         songs from Shakespeare's plays.  The rhymes and
         jingles became popular.

One:     Some of the rhymes appear to have no meaning
         but others are associated with real people and
         historical events.

Two:     Old King Cole, for example, is said to have been
         a popular king of Britain in 200 A.D. He seems to
         have loved music.  His daughter was supposedly
         a skilled musician.

Aesop:   I am Aesop, a Greek slave who lived about 600 B.C.
         I told fables.  Fables are stories that have a lesson
         to teach or moral advice to give.

Authority: Aesop's fables use animals which talk, act, and think
         like humans.  They deal with human problems.

One:     Some say that Aesop collected stories and some say
         he made them up.  The important thing is that these
         stories have been collected and handed down from
         one generation to the next.

Two:     A Greek by the name of Demetrius Phalereus
         gathered about 200 of the tales into a collection
         called the Assemblies of Aesopic Tales.

Authority: This collection was translated into Latin about
         300 years later.  The Aesop tales have been combined
         with tales of other countries.  They are told and retold
         but they never lose their original moral or storyline.

Aesop:   We've heard enough talk from authorities and
         storytellers.  You and I are among the oldest
         storytellers.  Let us visit together.

Goose:    Yes, Aesop, we shall talk together.  Although I must say, you sound like a rather serious type of guy.

Aesop:    Why do you say that?  I like a joke.
I laugh at the foibles of people.

Goose:    That's my point.  You notice people's faults and point them out to us.  We don't always like that.

Aesop:    How about your rhymes?  Are you saying that everybody is happy in your nursery rhymes?

Goose:    No, I guess they aren't.  But you admit
that you find fault with people.

Aesop:    Let us put aside this conversation about personal faults and human frailty.  Let's talk about our stories.  Of everything you've written, which story is your favorite?

Goose:    I like most of them but I do have favorites.
"Pease Porridge Hot" is a favorite.  The lines
are short.  Children can clap their hands
while reciting it.  It's a favorite.

Aesop:    I suppose the "Hare and the Tortoise" is my favorite.
The hare, or rabbit, was always bragging about
how fast he was.  He was fast but he also took
frequent naps.  And while the hare was napping,
the slow-and-steady tortoise won the race.

Goose:    Little Miss Muffet was eating curds and whey.
A spider came by her and she ran away.
That rhyme has been discussed many times.

Aesop:    I understand why.  In years gone past, it was
expected that girls would be frightened by spiders.
But many girls are not afraid of spiders.

**Goose:**   I've been called bad names by feminists who say I painted a bad picture of females - like Little Miss Muffet and the Queen of Hearts. Other disagreeable characters are Contrary Mary, the Old Woman in a Shoe, and the farmer's wife who cut off the tails of mice.

**Aesop:**   As stories are handed down from one generation to the next, they are interpreted in different ways. People remain much the same but society's reactions and values change.

**Goose:**   I like your story about the goose that laid a golden egg. That poor goose. I feel sorry for her. She died in your story.

**Aesop:**   The man who owned the goose wanted the goose to lay more golden eggs than one a day. So he killed the goose to look for more gold inside of her.

**Goose:**   Poor goose and stupid man. He didn't understand that eggs take time to develop. When he killed the goose that laid the golden egg, he killed the best possession he had. People can be stupid.

**Aesop:**   And that's what my stories pointed out. They advised people to be happy with what they had - like my story about the city mouse and the country mouse.

**Goose:**   Your stories taught lessons. But I am particularly proud of my rhymes that filled children with a sense of wonder and imagination.

**Aesop:**   Which Mother Goose rhymes suggest wonder or imagination?

**Goose:**   "Twinkle, twinkle little star" suggests to children that they should look into the universe and wonder what is there, to dream of lands beyond what they can see.

**Aesop:**   My stories face harsh realities - like the story that tells people to beware of a wolf in sheep's clothing.

One:    Storytellers tell many stories.  Some are meant to entertain, some to warn, and some to make you feel good about who you are, and where you live.

Two:    All storytellers watch human nature.  This has been true from ancient times past up to the present.

Authority:    And it will continue. Thank you, Mother Goose. Thank you, Aesop.  Come see us again.

Goose & Aesop:    Thank you, we will come again.  And in the meantime, find our stories in your library.  I know we are there.

*The End*

# U.S. Presidential Trivia

*Cast:*

> *Quiz Master (this person asks the questions)*
> *Trivia Whiz One*
> *Trivia Whiz Two*
> *Trivia Whiz Three*

*Modifications you may wish to make:*
> *As presidents are elected, add information.*
> *Reassign the lines of one, two, & three to accommodate more readers.*

**Master:**  Welcome to the U.S. Presidents' Trivia Game.
I'll ask the questions.  Respond if you know the answer.

**One:**  I'm ready to go.

**Two:**  What are we waiting for?

**Three:**  Let the contest begin!

**Master:**  Who was the only president to receive a doctorate?

**One:**  Woodrow Wilson. And 9 presidents did
not go to college at all.

**Master:**  Just answer the questions.

**One:**  O.K. but I like to say what I know.

**Master:**  Who were the tallest and the shortest president?

**Two:**  Abraham Lincoln was 6' 4" - the tallest.
James Madison was 5' 4" - the shortest.

**Master:**  Which president was an orphan and who was adopted?

**Three:**  Herbert Hoover was an orphan and Gerald Ford was adopted.

**Master:**  Were any presidents the only child of the family?

| | |
|---|---|
| <u>Three:</u> | No. Many came from big families. |
| <u>Master:</u> | Name at least three state capitals that are named after United States Presidents. |
| <u>One:</u> | I can name four: Madison, Wisconsin; Jefferson City, Missouri; Lincoln, Nebraska; and Jackson, Mississippi. |
| <u>Master:</u> | Who was the first to appear on television? |
| <u>Two:</u> | Herbert Hoover. |
| <u>Master:</u> | Who was the first to be married in the White House? |
| <u>Three:</u> | Grover Cleveland. |
| <u>Master:</u> | Who was called the "Philosopher of Democracy?" |
| <u>One:</u> | Thomas Jefferson. |
| <u>Master:</u> | Who was a successful peanut grower and entrepreneur? |
| <u>Two:</u> | Jimmy Carter. |
| <u>Master:</u> | Who was president during Operation Desert Storm? |
| <u>Three:</u> | George Bush. |
| <u>Master:</u> | Which states are named after presidents? |
| <u>One:</u> | Only one - the state of Washington. |
| <u>Master:</u> | How many presidents were assassinated while in office? Who were they? |
| <u>Two:</u> | Four were assassinated. They were Lincoln, Garfield, McKinley and Kennedy. |
| <u>Master:</u> | Whose final words were "Please put out the light"? |
| <u>Three:</u> | Theodore Roosevelt's. |

**Master:**    Which president is buried in Abilene, Kansas?

**One:**    Dwight Eisenhower.

**Master:**    Who served the shortest and the longest times as president?

**Two:**    Benjamin Harrison served 32 days, and Franklin
Roosevelt served 12 years and 39 days.

**Master:**    Which president could have been described as -
six feet tall, over 300 pounds, with deep-set
eyes and turned-up mustache?

**Three:**    William Howard Taft.

**Master:**    Name two presidents with military careers.

**One:**    Ulysses Grant and Dwight Eisenhower.

**Master:**    Which president could be described as the first President
born in North Carolina, a graduate of Princeton University,
and a minister to Russia?

**Two:**    James Polk.

**Master:**    "Thomas Jefferson still survives" were the last
words of which president?

**Three:**    John Adams.

---

> *--- optional ---insert*
> *Find other facts about presidents.  Add the information here.*

---

**Master:**    This concludes our game of U.S. Presidential Trivia Game.
Thanks for being with us today.

*The End*

# Women Artists

*Cast*
  *Artist - represents all artists*
  *General Public One*
  *General Public Two*
  *General Public Three*
  *Museum Curator*
  *Museum Guide*

*Modifications you may wish to make:*
  *Add information about other artists: males, other female artists,*
    *local artists, artists from your geographic area.*
  *The lines for the Artist may be assigned to more than one reader.*
  *Display "plate books" showing artists' pictures. Add information*
    *about the artists shown in the books.*

**Curator:** Welcome to the art museum. "Female Artists" is
the subject for this exhibit. We hope you enjoy it.

**Guide:** Please follow me as we view the works of
well-known and not-so-well-known artists.

**Artist:** I feel compelled to make this statement. We,
as female artists, do not want our work to be
judged and valued - only because we are female.

**One:** Thank you for clarifying that position.

**Curator:** Each of the works may stand alone.
They are combined into one exhibit the same
way other exhibits are arranged around a theme.

**Guide:** The first two works are done by Miriam Shapiro.
She was born in Toronto, Canada. She is
a printmaker and Abstract Expressionist painter.
We are fortunate to have her works.

**Artist:** In the early 1970s, I experimented with bits of
household items - like towels, lace, and colorful
fabrics. These were combined into vibrant active
pictures of people. I often show people dancing.

**Two:** Shapiro's works reflect an enthusiasm for life.

**Guide:** Our next artist is Mary Cassatt. She painted pictures of many people but her pictures of women and children have earned her the most attention.

**Three:** Cassatt's paintings show women who are feminine and caring. The children look as if they could be held and hugged.

**Guide:** As a painter, Mary Cassatt is grouped with the Impressionists.

**Artist:** I am the next artist and I wish to introduce myself. My name is Janet Fish. For as long as I can remember, I have been fascinated by what I saw reflected through glass - glass vases and dishes.

**One:** Did anyone teach you how to paint these reflections? How did you learn to paint the objects, and then the same image as seen through glass?

**Artist:** There are many things you can learn from teachers. But there are other things you must learn on your own. The things you learn on your own are the artistic expressions that make your work special.

**Two:** If I could afford an original painting, I'd buy a Janet Fish. I'd hang it in the lobby of my business. Your paintings are colorful and satisfying.

**Artist:** Thank you. It is words of praise that keep me creating glass containers and the objects in or near them.

**Guide:** Janet Fish is a Yale graduate. Her paintings are growing in popularity. Her colors are strong but gentle.

**Curator:** Please allow me to explain the next piece - the painting of bamboo. It is a very old painting - from 13th century China.

**Three:** How can paintings of that age be preserved?

**Curator:**  Special techniques and much care make it possible. The artist who painted this picture of bamboo was Kuan Tao-Sheng. She and her husband worked for the Mongol emperor, Kublai Khan.

**Artist:**  The emperor required much writing. My husband and I did that. But my real love was painting the bamboo plant that is an important part of China.

**Guide:**  We move from Kuan Tao-Sheng of 13th century China to Grandma Moses of 20th century America. Grandma Moses is the folk artist recognized by almost everyone. Her paintings show busy rural life - with people working and relaxing.

**Artist:**  I painted whole landscapes with many people. Whole landscapes show the vastness of open spaces. The people show cooperation with the environment and with each other.

**Guide:**  Grandma Moses did not start to paint until she was in her seventies.

**One:**  This next painting looks something like the works of Mary Cassatt. It looks Impressionistic.

**Guide:**  The painting is Impressionistic. It is done by the French painter Berthe Morisot. Her style shows people or objects blending with their environment.

**Artist:**  In my time, most artists painted indoors. I wanted to paint outdoors so that I could see true colors and have maximum light. And because I wanted to do it, I did.

**Two:**  I recognize this next work of art. It is one of Georgia O'Keeffe's "bone" pictures. O'Keeffe painted bones, flowers, and landscapes of the southwest.

**Guide:**  This is an O'Keeffe. Many people recognize works of O'Keeffe. They are recognized because she received much publicity, and because she is the only one to specialize in paintings of bones and huge flowers that fill the whole canvas.

Curator:    We move to the next section of the exhibit.  This
            section features sculptures.  Faith Ringgold's quilts
            are included in this section.

Guide:      Faith Ringgold is best known for her large quilts
            which represent a theme.

Artist:     "Sonny's Quilt" is a tribute to Sonny Rollins,
            a jazz saxophonist. "Tar Beach Quilt" represents
            my childhood memories.

Three:      "Tar Beach Quilt" shows children sleeping on the roof,
            parents visiting with friends, the outline of the George
            Washington Bridge, and stars shining overhead.

One:        There are words on the quilt.  What do they say?

Artist:     They tell the story of the quilt. I thought my
            childhood to be a wonderful childhood because
            of all I could see and feel from the rooftop.

Guide:      The next art piece represents the artist's political
            and emotional views.  This is the work of Marisol
            Escobar.  Escobar was born in Paris. Her parents
            were from Venezuela.  She lived in Europe, South
            America and the United States.

Artist:     I started out as a painter but later switched to
            mixed-media assemblages which voiced an
            opinion about American institutions.

Two:        This next work has to be the work of Louise Nevelson.
            I recognize her style: dull black sculpture made from
            objects found in the environment.

Guide:      Very good. Louise Nevelson was of Russian descent.
            She was six when the family came to America.  She's
            known for her many black, white, or gold assemblages.

Three:      I recognize this last item as a copy of the Abraham
            Lincoln statue in the United States Capitol. Was
            this sculpted by a woman?  Is that why it is here?

**Guide:**       Yes. Vinnie Ream Hoxie was only 18 years of age when she was commissioned to make this 6' 11" statue.  She won the commission because of a model of Lincoln she had made.

**Artist:**      I lived during the Civil War.  A few months before Lincoln was assassinated, I had the opportunity to personally see him.  While others listened to what he was saying, I sculpted a model of the president.

**Guide:**       Vinnie Hoxie used this model as an example of what her talent was.  Since she had personally seen the president, and had a working model of him, she was given the commission.

> *--- optional insert --*
> *add other information here.*

**Curator:**     Thank you for visiting our exhibit of women artists. I urge you to support the work of all artists.

**Guide:**       This completes our tour.  Have a good day.

*The End*

# Women Who Supported Causes

*Cast*

> *Reporter*
> *Clara Barton*
> *Sophonisba Breckinridge*
> *Mother Teresa*
> *Harriet Tubman*
> _____ *(add names, if you added information - see last page of play)*

*Modifications you may wish to make*

> *Names of the women, and the causes supported, may be listed on cards.*
> Clara  Barton  - Founded the Red Cross.
> Sophonisba Breckinridge - Improved Social Work
> Mother Teresa - Helped Society's Outcasts
> Harriet Tubman - Lead Slaves to Freedom
> _____ (add names, if you added information - s ee last page of play)

| | |
|---|---|
| <u>Reporter</u>: | Welcome to our theater.  Our guests today are Clara Barton, Mother Teresa, Harriet Tubman, Sophonisba Breckinridge. *( add names - if you added information - see last page of play)*. Each will introduce herself. |
| <u>Clara Barton</u>: | My name is Clara Barton. I founded the Red Cross. |
| <u>Mother Teresa</u>: | My name is Mother Teresa. I serve society's outcasts. |
| <u>Harriet Tubman</u>: | I am Harriet Tubman. I led my people to freedom. |
| <u>Breckinridge</u>: | I am Sophonisba Breckinridge. I contributed to the field of social work. |
| | _____ *(Add names - if you added information - see last page of play)* |
| <u>Reporter</u>: | My first question is directed to Clara Barton. Why did you start the Red Cross? |

| | |
|---|---|
| <u>Clara Barton</u>: | It happened during the Civil War. I took it upon myself to bring supplies to the battlefields. After the war, I formed a group to search for missing persons. |
| <u>Reporter</u>: | How did the Red Cross become such an effective organization? |
| <u>Clara Barton</u>: | It took much cooperation and persistence. Governments around the world had to be convinced that a world-wide organization would serve people during war and peace. |
| <u>Reporter</u>: | Thank you, Clara Barton, for founding the Red Cross.  The symbol, the red cross, tells the world of its mission.  Your efforts are appreciated. |
| <u>Clara Barton</u>: | It's been a pleasure to be here.  Continue to support and use the Red Cross.  It serves all people in need. |
| <u>Reporter</u>: | Our next guest is Mother Teresa, friend of the very poor and society's outcasts. Mother Teresa, why did you start a religious order to help people in Calcutta? |
| <u>Mother Teresa</u>: | Calcutta was the city that changed my life. The needs of the very poor called to me. They needed food, medicine, and love. |
| <u>Reporter</u>: | How did you become interested in Calcutta? |
| <u>Mother Teresa</u>: | I was a member of a religious group.  My superiors sent me to Calcutta.  My job was to teach religion. But teaching was not to be my main work. |
| <u>Reporter</u>: | You started your own religious group to serve the poor, sick, and hungry.  Hospitals were your main focus.  Is that correct? |
| <u>Mother Teresa</u>: | Hospitals were the first to be established.  But soon we also operated schools, orphanages, youth centers, and shelters for lepers and the dying. |

Reporter:

You were awarded the Nobel Peace Prize in 1979. How did you feel about that honor?

Mother Teresa:

The award gave further evidence that the needs of the poor, sick, hungry and dying have nothing to do with politics. They are problems of humanity. I serve humanity - not governments. The Nobel Peace Prize affirmed that. I was humbled by the honor.

Reporter:

The world extends its thanks and appreciation to you and your sisters.

Mother Teresa:

Wherever you are, consider the needs of people.

Reporter:

Thank you, Mother Teresa, for being with us today. *(slight pause)* Our next guest is Harriet Tubman. Harriet helped black people escape to freedom by means of the Underground Railroad. Harriet, how was this possible?

Harriet Tubman:

The Underground Railroad was not a railroad - with cars and tracks. It was a path or route to territory in which slaves could be free. There were stops along the railroad - homes, barns, sheds, and people who would help slaves reach lands where slaves were free.

Reporter:

You, personally, escaped to freedom. Then you made several trips back into the slave states to lead others to freedom. Weren't you afraid?

Harriet Tubman:

I was very much afraid. But I was also determined that my people should be free. It was worth the risk.

Reporter:

When you were 13, your skull was fractured because you angered a supervisor. Did you bear any lifelong effects of that injury?

Harriet Tubman:

Yes. I would faint - black out - from time to time. Other than that, I was all right.

Reporter:

Was there any one event that was particularly scary? If "yes," how did you deal with it?

*Vol. Two* - **98**

Readers' Theate. WOMEN WHO SUPPORTED CAUSES page 4

Harriet Tubman: The time I was most frightened was when I was leading slaves to freedom. I saw my slave master walking towards me. I had to think fast.

Reporter: What did you do?

Harriet Tubman: I had just bought some chickens. I let the chickens go. We chased the chickens. This made it impossible for the slave master and slave hunters to see us clearly and to identify us.

Reporter: You served the Union Army during the Civil War. What services did you give?

Harriet Tubman: I was a nurse, scout, and spy for the Union Army.

Reporter: And after the war, what did you do?

Harriet Tubman: I helped raise money for black schools and a home for elderly blacks who had no place to go. It was known as Harriet Tubman Home. It was in Auburn, New York.

Reporter: Thank you, Harriet. *(to audience)* In 1978, a U.S. postage stamp with Tubman's portrait was issued. *(slight pause).* Our next guest is Sophonisba Breckinridge. You are considered a pioneer in the field of social work. Why?

Breckinridge: After I graduated from Wellesley College in 1888, I went to law school and became Kentucky's first female lawyer. I joined the University of Chicago's faculty in 1904.

Reporter: When did you begin championing the cause of social work?

Breckinridge: Social workers had been traditionally trained by reading books. I believed that social workers had to study from books but also should work directly in the community. Direct contact with people and civil organizations is the best training for social workers.

| | |
|---|---|
| Reporter: | You started the School of Social Service Administration in 1920. Why is this important? |
| Breckinridge: | When a university establishes a special school to teach and study a field, the graduates in that field receive the best training possible. I also established a magazine called the *Social Service Review*. |
| Reporter: | A magazine makes it possible for social workers in all parts of the world to share information about recent developments in the field. |
| Breckinridge: | My efforts joined with the efforts of others to establish that governments must take an active part in helping the needy. That attitude continues. |
| Reporter: | Thank you for being with us today and for your pioneer efforts in social works. |

---

*---- optional insert ---*
*Add other information about people who supported causes.*
*Format: the reporter introduces and asks the first question.*
*The person responds. There may be one or several*
*lines of dialogue.*

*If you add information here, add introductions to the*
*opening lines also.*

---

| | |
|---|---|
| Clara Barton: | Each of us responded to a need of our time. |
| Mother Teresa: | We served people who were not able - at the moment - to help themselves. |
| Harriet Tubman: | We supported the belief that each living person has a right to respect and freedom. |
| Breckinridge: | Our contributions gave our lives a sense of fulfillment. And, in so doing, we helped others. |
| Reporter: | Thank you for being with us today. Our play is ended. |

*The End*

# *Index of Persons Referenced*

# Index of Persons Referenced

## *Communication with the Author*

**Mail to:** Leadership Publishers Inc. P.O. Box 8358 Des Moines, Iowa 50301- 8358

My comment refers to:
    ❑ plays - in general
    ❑ specific play:

      Title _____

      _____ pp. _____

Comment(s):

_____

_____

_____

_____

_____

_____

_____

_____

_____

                    ❑ continues on other side

*If you wish the author to respond to your comments, include your name & address.*

Name_____ Position_____

School/Organization_____

Address_____

City_____ State_____ Zip_____-_____

# Request

**Mail to:** Leadership  Publishers Inc.    P.O. Box 8358    Des Moines, Iowa  50301- 8358

*Please send:*

❑ *Information on in-service by Dr. Lois Roets* (author of these plays).
> *Inservice is available for these plays & related topics:*
> ___ *language arts / reading teachers,*
> ___ *librarians,*
> ___ *educators / parents of gifted & talented,*
> ___ *counselors (who use these plays as forum of review),*
> ___ *social studies teachers,*
> ___ *vocational / business teachers,*
> ___ *students - of "all of the above".*

_____ *Other specific topics:* _____

_____

_____

_____

❑ *Sample play from* - (please include 2 first-class stamps for each sample requested)
___*Vol. One:* **General Interest**
___*Vol. Two:* **Famous People**
___*Vol. Three:* **Entrepreneurs**

❑ *Send catalog and add me to the mailing list.*

Name_____ Position_____

School / Organization _____

Address_____

City _____ State_____ Zip_____-_____

# Educators:

## Ours is a great profession.

### We are the

## molders of minds

### and

## sharers of dreams.

### And

## in the process,

## we, also, are changed.